IF YOU KNEW...

...WHO YOU WERE, YOU COULD BE WHO YOU ARE !

YOUR PERSONAL CAREER PROFILE

GERALD M. STURMAN Ph.D.

Senior Technical Advisor
BARRY LUSTIG, M.A. NCCC
Director, Professional Development Institute
Federated Employment & Guidance Service
New York, NY

 Bierman House • Bedford, N

"If you knew who you were...
you could be who you are!"

Comprehensive Personal Career Profile®

Personal Career Profile®

©1989, 1990, 1991, 1992 by Bierman House, Inc.
19 Brookwood Road
Bedford, NY 10506
(914) 234-3200

ISBN 0-9626887-0-3

[√] *Contents*

[√] *Preface*

*P*eople, as in all things in nature, are unique and grow in many directions. Each of us is born with a set of genes unlike any others and into a family and a time in history and a place on the planet different from any other human being. It is not surprising, therefore, that everyone deals differently with the world and responds to complex relationships with people and things in a way that no one else does.

The One And Only You

*A*s we grow and change, the people and things and events around us and the way we respond to them contribute to shaping our lives. At any one moment in our personal histories, we are a complex and specific collection of thoughts, ideas, emotions, experiences, feelings, skills, interests, personal qualities, likes and dislikes, behavioral tendencies, personality traits, tastes, stylistic preferences, passions, aptitudes, intellectual orientations, physical coordination, and more. Some of these things are clear to us. Many of them are often buried under the surface of our lives, unrealized and unexamined. Yet, we do seem to want to know ourselves.

"The urge to experience and define personal identity must be genetic, woven into the human DNA, because it is a driving force that has motivated people throughout all history. In the search for some understanding of themselves, some sense of who they are in the universe, human beings repeatedly ask, Who am I? Why am I the way I am? Who can I become? In what direction should I go? How can I change? Why am I here?...No other human being can give any one of us 'The Answers.' We need to find those answers for ourselves, and they seldom come fast, simple, or tidy (except maybe in retrospect). We are always 'piecing it together,' as long as we live." (**The Creative Brain,** *Ned Herrmann, Brain Books ©1988.)*

If You Knew Who You Were... You Could Be Who You Are!

*W*hat can we hope to get from a better understanding of who we are? Think of a time when you learned something new. Not just a single fact, but a whole field of knowledge or a skill – math or chemistry or English literature or American history, or a language, or a musical instrument, or how to paint a picture (or a house), or how your car works, or any other large and complex set of ideas or techniques, or skills. When you first started, the task seemed massive and each new thing was learned with some effort. It looked as if it would never be possible to be any good at it. You got discouraged, but you stayed with it for one reason or another. And then one day, in a moment of sudden renewed vitality, you discovered that the thing you were struggling with had begun to flow out of you with clarity and control. You had mastered the subject and could now begin to work with it in useful ways. You had reached a threshold of understanding that gave you power.

Power is the ability to get things done – to take action and transform undifferentiated raw material into recognizable reality. The raw materials can be physical, or they can be abstractions such as ideas or symbols or emotions. Knowledge is power. When you know, you can begin to act appropriately and effectively, rather than unconsciously and blindly. With self knowledge you are more likely to be able to create what you want, rather than settle for what arrives accidentally. The power to travel to a foreign country and speak the language in a way that you can get what you want when you go into a store or a restaurant is satisfying and fulfilling. Fumbling around and settling for fish when you wanted to eat filet is frustrating and leaves you feeling powerless.

Personal power is the ability to have your life be the way you want it to be. People often say, "I want to be myself, I want to be who I am." But, how can you be who you are, if you don't have enough knowledge to know who you are? If you don't have the knowledge, you don't have the power. And, if you don't have the power, you can't get what you want.

Work and Self-Expression

*T*hink of all the different places where we say we are "working." At home, we do the dishes, clean the house, repair broken things, mow the lawn, plant flowers, paint rooms, and do all the other things that we call "working around the house." When we do these things we are contributing something of positive value to our home environment. In our communities, we work on fund drives and election campaigns, and give our time to the local scouts and ball clubs, and attend PTA meetings. Again, we are contributing something of value to our communities. In our jobs, we were hired because we were expected to bring some value to the company for which we work and, either consciously or unconsciously, that is exactly what we strive to do. So, work has something to do with contributing value.

Where does that value come from? The answer comes from looking at the common denominator in all of the examples above – that is, the value comes from us, the contributor. When we say that something comes from us, we mean that it comes from our minds and bodies and activities. The contribution of value comes from what we do which in turn comes from who we are. It is clear, therefore, that...

"Work is the expression of self in the contribution of value."

What we are doing when we work is expressing ourselves by contributing value outward from ourselves into the world. Work is a form of self-expression. Given that we spend the major portion of our lives working, our overall experience of self-expression is enormously influenced by our worklives. Truly satisfied people are fully self-expressive. Full self-expression means being able to take what is naturally within us and transform it into a satisfying reality outside of us. Because self-expression is a creative process of transformation, it requires power to make it happen effectively. Fully self-expressive people are, by definition, powerful people. The world around them is the way they make it. They are the proactive, responsible, satisfied, energized masters of their own lives.

If work is about self-expression, and full self-expression is about power, and power in this context is about self-knowledge, it makes sense that to the extent that we have a deep level of self knowledge we can be more powerful and self-expressive at work and therefore more satisfied. Unfortunately, many people are not satisfied in their worklives. When they talk about their jobs they use terms like "frustrated," "powerless," "angry," "bored" – not what you would expect to hear from people who are fully self-expressive.

To be satisfied in your job, you have to be doing work you like to do in an environment you like to be in, with the kinds of people you like to be around, interacting with the job and the environment and the people in ways that are consistent with who you are.

To know who you are and to be who you are is the ultimate form of self-expression and power. To the extent that you do know who you are, your work, career, and life choices are more likely to lead you to a more fully self-expressive worklife – a life of more satisfaction, contribution, and joy.

Acknowledgments

Experts in career development and psychological assessment have been crossing paths for many years, and there have been many contributors across the disciplines. The importance of style and psychological type as an indicator of appropriate career choice and of work satisfaction must be recognized by any serious worker in the career development field, and a deep debt of gratitude is owed to Katharine C. Briggs and Isabel Briggs Myers for bringing us the beauty of their deep appreciation of the work of Jung and its application to such a wide range of human experience. The work of Consulting Psychologists Press, the Association for Psychological Type, and the Center for Applications of Psychological Type for spreading the ideas of Myers and Briggs are also acknowledged.

The career development field has its own share of skillful and creative contributors. Among those pioneers whose writings have been especially useful to the work included in this book are John L. Holland, Edgar H. Schein, and Richard N. Bolles. My own involvement in the career development field comes from a long and fruitful association with Tom Jackson and his creative contributions to our understanding of the world of work.

I would also like to acknowledge with appreciation the following career development specialists and professional friends and colleagues who read the manuscript and offered helpful suggestions – Rose Arant, Jack Ballard, Joanna Chaleff, Jill Conner, Mitzi Gregory, Margaret Jacobs, Naomi Kapp, Ken Kraus, Nettie Kraus, Marianna Maddocks, John Maddocks, Linda Maldonado, Ken McCoy, John Reed, Sonia Scheim, and Daralee Schulman. Additional acknowledgments are due to the Federation Employment & Guidance Service for negotiating so generously for Barry Lustig's time; to my colleague and friend Breese White whose knowledge of career development was earned in the corporate trenches and who generously contributed his wisdom and spirit to this work; to my very good friend David Palmer who applied his professional skill and judgment to the editing and chore; to Mary Ed Porter who did the final editing and proofreading; to my colleague Karen Cooney who patiently and painstakingly gave great amounts of her own time to enter this book into the computer; and to my wife and partner, Peggy Bier, who supported the long hours of research and my attachment to a word processor through the many drafts with her enthusiasm for the project, common-sense approach to our work, and loving sacrifice of our valuable time together on nights and weekends.

The heart and soul of this book have been inspired by the genius and lifelong dedication of Barry Lustig. I was introduced to Barry by Bill Murray, one of his students, who thought that we might find some kind of work to do together. I have been designing, developing, and delivering various kinds of career development workshops to major corporations for many years, and have always been struck by the fact that although assessment tools exist in many forms, there is no one place to go for a comprehensive approach to career assessment, unless you pay a professional counselor to take you through a battery of tests. Even then, you could not be assured of getting all the right instruments. I suggested to Barry that I would like to develop something truly comprehensive that could be completely self-administered, without a counselor, or computers, and with immediate feedback. Barry leaped into the task with overwhelming enthusiasm and energy and buried me in books, papers, and enormously energizing dialogues on career assessment, career development, worklife satisfaction, job-person fit, psychological type, career type, and every other imaginable aspect of people and their worklives. He is a walking encyclopedia of knowledge in the career field and read every word of every draft and insisted on clarity, comprehensiveness, and perfection. The way this book is organized, the material selected for inclusion, the tone, and the usefulness are all due to Barry's ability and commitment to the field. My role was to put it into readable and workable form. Anything that doesn't work is my responsibility. Everything that does work is because of Barry Lustig.

X

Gerald M. Sturman
Woodstock, NY
August, 1989

*H*ow many people do you know who can honestly say... *"I'm really excited about my job!"*...? Can *you* say it with a clear conscience? There can't be many people who can. Surveys show that up to 80 percent of the people working in this country are dissatisfied or mismatched in their jobs. It's too bad, because we put in a few thousand hours a year, and work about 100 thousand hours before we retire. What a waste, what a loss, and how sad it is to spend a lifetime doing work that's not exciting or satisfying or self-expressive, or what we really want to be doing.

Are You Excited About Your Job?

*B*ut why are so many people dissatisfied at work? The clear and obvious answer is that many people are not doing the job that's most natural for them. Many people don't fit in the jobs they are in. If you examine the way people get their jobs, you can see why. They come out of school, look over the field, and take the best looking job that comes along. They think it might suit them · because the pay is good, or the working conditions seem nice, or the commute is short, or the benefits are good, or a relative works there, or there's not much else around! Very few people get into the jobs they are in because they are really certain about what they want to do, know for sure what environment really suits their personality and way of working and learning, what kind of boss and colleagues they can work best with, how their skills and personal qualities can best be used to do what kinds of jobs, what skills they like to use the most, what their values are and how those determine what kinds of jobs they should be in, and so on.

So they get into these jobs more or less by accident or by the action of external factors, and the rest of their working lives follow a pattern:

Jobs don't seem to be "natural." People use skills they don't care about and have to wait for the weekend to use the skills that turn them on. They use their minds too much and their hands too little or vice versa. They work in big companies when a small organization would suit them better, or they are stuck behind a desk when they would really shine if they were out meeting people. They become managers when they are really happier in the laboratory, and they keep on doing secretarial work when they would love to be managing projects and people. They work on teams when they would rather be individual contributors, and they try to become entrepreneurs when they really need the security of an organization. They struggle under the yoke of a big organization and a hierarchy of bosses when they would be happy as clams running their own business and making decisions that really count. They try to get ahead in their company but don't seem to know enough about what they have to contribute (that anyone would find useful enough) to move them up the ladder.

1

Or, they do get ahead, and as they get higher and higher they get less and less satisfied with the hours and the pace and the responsibility and the pressure; and the money and the title seem to matter less and less. So they go from job to job, or from one career to another seeking success and satisfaction and never really finding either one. The dream seems to have faded. Something seems to be missing.

Is any of this familiar to you? Are you sure about what you want and what kind of a working life would be most satisfying to you, or can you see yourself in this pattern now, or drifting in this direction?

You Can Break the Pattern — The Importance of Self-Assessment

*T*his book is intended to help you break the pattern of dissatisfaction at work by allowing you to discover who you really are and what is the best thing for you to do to build a worklife that is most natural for you and satisfying. Three major accomplishments available to you here as a result of going through this assessment process include:

1. You will develop a clearer understanding of your personality type, what motivates you, and what skills you want to use in your work. This deeper self-knowledge will enhance your self-acceptance and self-esteem.

2. You will be able to make more informed and suitable job and career decisions by having a more systematic way of considering the major variables related to career success and satisfaction.

3. You will gain greater insight into your developmental needs – areas in which you need to improve your personal and professional effectiveness so that you can have what you want in your work and life.

Who Are You?

*T*here are four basic and broad elements that define who you are in relation to your worklife:

1. Your **Style**… In what ways do you prefer to relate to the world? How do you like to work? What kind of work environment do you prefer? What are your preferred methods of communication? What is your preferred management and/or leadership style? What are the appropriate contributions for you to make to an organization? How do you relate to people and what kinds of bosses and colleagues and subordinates do you work best around?

2. Your **Motivation**…What needs, interests, values, and beliefs determine what you like to do? What is most important for you to retain in your worklife? What motivates you to do your best work? What kind of work do you really want to do, and what is it that you don't want to do? What do

you want to put into your work and what do you want to get out of it? What motivates you to do your best work?

3. Your **Skills**...What are you able to do? What are the things that you can do that you would really like to do? What skills can you take with you wherever you go? What skills do you most want to use in your work?

4. Your **Internal Barriers and Developmental Needs**....What is it that blocks you from getting what you want out of your worklife? What attitudes, opinions, beliefs, or behavior patterns keep you from experiencing success and satisfaction or from performing as effectively as you would need to or want to? From a clear understanding of the first three elements and your internal barriers, you will be better able to derive your *Developmental Needs*. That is, what would you like to be able to do or need to do better or differently that will allow you to make full use of your potential?

The four elements are not independent of each other and are interwoven into the pattern of your life and career. Each component interacts with the others. Your style is one of the determinants of your motivation and the skills you have chosen to develop. Your motivation also determines what skills you have developed as well as those you choose to use and perfect. Things at which you are naturally skilled contribute to your motivation, and so on.

These four basic elements will tell you a lot about what you need to know to create a more effective and satisfying worklife and career. The rest will be up to you. You can go as far as you want in the career planning process, and the next to last chapter of this book will give you some suggested ways of using what you have learned here. There is also a considerable amount of reading you can do to learn more about yourself and about career and life planning. A bibliography of support materials is provided in the final chapter.

Elements of Effective Career Assessment

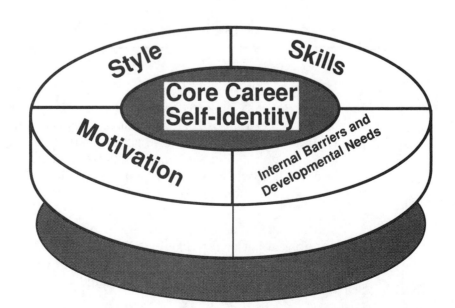

The Process

*S*tarting in the next chapter, you will proceed through a series of assessments. Each of these assessments represents a piece of the whole – style, motivation, needs, internal barriers, or developmental needs. When you have completed the assessments, you will be instructed in the completion of a *Personal Career Profile*. This profile will allow you to gather all of the work you have done into a coherent, readable, and understandable picture of yourself in relationship to your worklife and career. This profile can then be used in whatever career planning process you choose to follow, whether it's on your own, with a professional counselor, or in a workshop run by your company, or in any other type of career planning course. Self assessment is the foundation of good career management, and your planning should not proceed until this process is complete and you have expanded your clarity about yourself. Having completed this process, you will be much clearer about your career planning needs and will be able to produce more effective results for yourself.

Organization of the Chapters

*E*ach assessment chapter of this profile is organized in the same way:

1. A brief introduction to the particular element to be assessed in the chapter.

2. Instructions in using the assessment tool.

3. The assessment tool.

4. Instructions for scoring the assessment.

5. A scoring form.

6. A description of the results of the different possible scores.

Discovering Who You Are

*T*he trip into yourself on which you are about to embark is a voyage of discovery. Its purpose is to provide a systematic framework and tools to enable you to find out as much about yourself and your relationship to work and career as it is possible in this self-assessment format. Some of what you discover here will be useful in parts of your life other than work, and you will see the connections as you proceed.

It is important that you go through the entire process before you make any decisions about your worklife and career. You will be creating a *Personal Career Profile* at the end of the process which will help you to tie it all together. No one instrument here will tell you the whole story, which is why there are several different inventories and indicators that you will use. The final picture is only complete when the last brush stroke is in place. Patience will bring great rewards.

Take as much time as you need to complete the process. It does not all have to be done at a single sitting. Let your thoughts and feelings linger on some of the discoveries you make and move on only when you feel you are ready. Set the book aside for a few days if you need to think some things over, or another project begs for your attention. Come back refreshed and ready to do more work on yourself. The experience of being in the process over several days, or even weeks, can be valuable.

Also know that there will be rough waters and dangerous shoals. Sometimes self-discovery is a difficult process. Have no fear – you will reach your destination whole! And, you will complete the voyage very much energized by the experiences along the way and by the exciting potential for a more truly satisfying worklife that you can see clearly ahead. The results are well worth the effort.

Good luck, bon voyage, and happy sailing!

One thing you know for sure is that you're different from everyone else around you. Unless you have an identical twin you look different from everyone else. More importantly, you act differently.

You Are Unique

You think, talk, listen, and learn differently. You like a different collection of foods, flowers, animals, places, and music than anyone else. You have a different collection of friends and colleagues and relatives. You like to do a different set of things at work and at home and when you're out having a good time than anyone else. You relate differently. You communicate differently. You make up your mind differently. You tend to be outgoing or you're more on the reserved side. You're thoughtful or impulsive. You look at the world in a very down-to-earth, "just give me the facts" way, or you are intuitive and like to think about all the possibilities of how things might be. You have a whole set of preferences that are yours and yours alone. In short, you are a unique individual. There's no one on the planet exactly like you. There never was and never will be.

These individual differences make you special. They define your unique way of functioning in the world, and they allow you to make a unique contribution in the world.

Being Natural

This set of preferences or patterns is "naturally" yours. When you are the way you prefer to be, and act the way you prefer to act, you are being natural. Your way of being and your manner of acting feels natural. This is what it means to be natural – true to your own nature.

Your natural way of being can be approximately described by a set of characteristic preferences which taken together define your psychological type. Each type relates to the world differently. This form of relation to the world is called your style. No type or style is better than any other and each has its own pattern of strengths and weaknesses. Specific types tend to be drawn to certain careers, but research has shown that all types and styles can be found in all careers.

Assessing Your Work Type

*T*his assessment is designed to allow you to discover your preferred type or natural preferences of dealing with both your inner and outer worlds when you are at work. While the Myers-Briggs Type Indicator® (a registered trademark of Consulting Psychologists Press, Inc.) provides your overall psychological type across all of your life's activities, the assessment which you will do below is specifically oriented toward your working life. It is most important that you answer the questions from the point of view of how you *really* behave in the work situations described. Avoid thinking about the way you *wish* you preferred to behave, or think you ought to act, or think your boss would like you to act, in the situation. Think always - *"...this is the way I actually behave - this is how I think, or act, or decide, or choose in this situation."* Answer the questions as honestly and as objectively as possible. The closer you come to the truth about how you actually behave, the more useful the information will be to you.

Circle the letter (a) or (b) for the answer that is a more accurate description of how you most often act, think, or feel.

1. Do your best ideas at work come from
    a)   an interchange of ideas and sharing with others, or
    b)   quiet thought on your own?

2. When you run a meeting, are you usually
    a)   disciplined about following your prepared agenda, or
    b)   flexible and open to whatever comes up?

3. When handling a subordinate's development, would you be more likely to
    a)   discuss a problem you have with his or her behavior, or
    b)   dislike telling them unpleasant things?

4. Do you prefer the place where you work to be
    a)   structured with clear rules and regulations, or
    b)   more open-ended and laissez-faire?

5. Would you rather have a supervisor with whom you have
    a)   a lot of day-by-day interaction, or
    b)   only infrequent interaction?

6. Do you prefer meetings where most time is spent on
    a)   the application of the ideas discussed, or
    b)   the ideas themselves?

7. Do you prefer a work environment in which
    a)   frequent conflict breeds interesting discussions and ideas, or
    b)   harmony is valued and conflict is avoided?

8. Do you prefer projects at work
  a)   to be well defined and planned out, or
  b)   to allow for flexible interpretation?

9. Do you prefer to spend your lunch hour
  a)   eating with a group, or
  b)   eating alone or with one close colleague?

10. If your boss gives you a difficult task, do you usually
  a)   collect as much information as possible before starting, or
  b)   dive in and rely on your ability to work things out?

11. In a performance appraisal, would you prefer your boss to write
  a)   that you are intelligent and reasonable, or
  b)   that you are warm and personable?

12. Do you prefer to
  a)   plan your work day carefully in advance, or
  b)   let the day progress and see how things turn out?

13. Do you more often prefer to keep your office door
  a)   open, or
  b)   closed?

14. When a new idea flashes into your mind, do you usually
  a)   like to test it carefully before you get excited, or
  b)   get excited and want to follow through quickly?

15. In a team meeting, do you prefer to emphasize
  a)   an analytical discussion of the facts, or
  b)   a discussion of the values involved?

16. Do you prefer a job in which the rewards
  a)   are seen clearly in regular periods, or
  b)   stretched out over long periods of time?

17. Do you dress for work in a way that
  a)   other people notice and admire your clothing, or
  b)   blends in with the norm?

18. When you solve problems, are you more likely to
  a)   give most weight to the facts in front of you, or
  b)   explore the full range of possibilities?

19. If you have to confront colleagues or subordinates, are you usually
  a)   interested in making sure you give them the facts accurately, or
  b)   more interested in making sure you don't hurt their feelings?

20. Would you rather have a boss who
   a)   provides a lot of structure and organization, or
   b)   leaves you to do things however they work best for you?

21. Do you prefer most of your jobs at work to be
   a)   a continuing series of short tasks, or
   b)   long projects on which you can concentrate your efforts?

22. When you write a report, do you usually think first of
   a)   the details, or
   b)   the big picture?

23. When you hear a presentation from a colleague, are you more likely to be
   a)   openly and intellectually critical, or
   b)   careful in voicing your opinions, especially when you disagree?

24. Do you prefer your own office to be one in which
   a)   things are orderly, organized, and systematic, or
   b)   there is a creative array of projects, papers, and books?

25. When you have lunch with your colleagues, would you rather
   a)   talk about people, or
   b)   talk about ideas?

26. Would you rather that your boss trust you with
   a)   practical problems to solve, or
   b)   policy problems to solve?

27. When faced with a decision at work, do you prefer to
   a)   think things through, or
   b)   trust your gut feelings?

28. Do you prefer the work you do every day to
   a)   be more of an ongoing routine, or
   b)   have frequent changes in activities and schedules?

29. When you have to organize and run a meeting, do you more often
   a)   feel satisfied that you have the opportunity to lead, or
   b)   prefer that someone else had the responsibility?

30. If you were asked to prepare a strategic plan, would you be more likely to
   a)   emphasize what is practical now, or
   b)   orient the plan toward future possibilities?

31. When faced with a decision at work, do you usually
   a)   focus on the facts and figures above all, or
   b)   give careful attention to people's feelings?

32. When your boss gives you a new project, do you usually prefer
- **a)** a clear statement of what is expected, or
- **b)** to be left to work it out the way you want?

33. Do you prefer to have
- **a)** a large group of colleagues at work, or
- **b)** a few colleagues that you know well?

34. In one-on-one meetings, are you more likely to?
- **a)** listen quietly and absorb details, or
- **b)** anticipate the speaker's words and interrupt?

35. If someone argues with a policy or decision you make, do you usually
- **a)** remain firm, or
- **b)** seek to avoid unpleasantness, anger, and disharmony?

36. When you have made a tough choice at work, are you usually
- **a)** satisfied that it is done, or
- **b)** wish that you could remain open to other alternatives?

37. When you attend a company outing, do you usually
- **a)** walk around and meet people you may not know well, or
- **b)** hang out with the colleagues you know best?

38. Do you think your colleagues see you more as a
- **a)** here and now person, or
- **b)** as someone with an orientation toward the future?

39. When you have a long and complex report to read, are you more likely to
- **a)** be patient and study the details, or
- **b)** try to get the general ideas and how you feel about them?

40. Do you prefer your work environment to be
- **a)** comfortable, predictable, and stable, or
- **b)** flexible and changing?

41. Would your colleagues at work more likely describe you as
- **a)** an energetic team player, or
- **b)** a quiet and thoughtful employee?

42. When you prepare a presentation, do you prefer to emphasize
- **a)** the use of real facts from your own experience, or
- **b)** the discussion of ideas and concepts?

43. Do you prefer to work with colleagues who
- **a)** rely heavily on logic, or
- **b)** look more often to their feelings?

44. If someone on your team is late with a scheduled task, are you usually
  a)   impatient and annoyed, or
  b)   open and flexible in stretching the deadlines?

45. When you attend a training session, are you more likely to
  a)   participate openly and actively, or
  b)   let others take the active role?

46. When colleagues and subordinates present ideas to you, are you more interested in
  a)   immediately useful ideas, or
  b)   ideas with innovative approaches?

47. If you have to deal with a colleague's feelings, do you prefer to be
  a)   truthful even if you can't be tactful, or
  b)   tactful, even if you can't tell the truth?

48. Do you prefer projects that
  a)   have a clear ending date when you know they will be finished, or
  b)   may remain open-ended to ensure that all bases are covered?

49. When you have a decision to make at work, do you more often
  a)   talk it over with a number of people before you decide, or
  b)   spend most of your time working it out in your own head?

50. Do you prefer a job where you can
  a)   use your experience to work at familiar tasks, or
  b)   confront ideas and problems that are new to you?

51. When you are at a meeting and a difference of opinion gets heated, do you usually
  a)   defend the side you think is most logical, or
  b)   try to create a harmonious atmosphere and solution?

52. If a colleague or subordinate comes to you to explain a difficulty in getting something done on time, do you usually
  a)   act impatiently, or
  b)   assist them in finding an approach that stretches the deadline?

53. Are you more interested in
  a)   the actual tasks you are doing day-by-day, or
  b)   the thoughts you have about your work?

54. When you attend a training session, do you usually prefer
  a)   experiential processes, or
  b)   information and abstractions?

55. When you have a meeting with a colleague, do you usually
  a) get through it quickly in a business-like manner, or
  b) linger over the sociable interaction?

56. Would you rather be in a job with
  a) activities requiring you to reach a conclusion, or
  b) activities that allow you to stay open to your experience?

57. When you ask a colleague for advice or help, are you more often
  a) comfortable, or
  b) somewhat ill at ease?

58. Are you more likely to
  a) remember facts presented in a meeting or report, or
  b) remember mostly the concepts presented?

59. When colleagues ask your advice about a work matter, do you more often
  a) help them make logical decision, or
  b) help them explore the values and policies in the situation?

60. When you are in a meeting, are you more interested in
  a) getting the job done, or
  b) making sure the way the job gets done is clearly understood?

61. When you are interrupted in the middle of a tough job, do you usually
  a) welcome the opportunity to talk to someone, or
  b) prefer to be left alone with your thoughts?

62. When you read a report, do you usually go first to
  a) the body of detailed information, or
  b) the summary or executive overview?

63. When you are putting forward a new idea at work, do you more often
  a) remain firm about the correctness of it, or
  b) try to persuade others by appealing to their sense of value?

64. If your boss insists that you schedule your work day, do you feel
  a) satisfied that you are organized, or
  b) uncomfortable that you are constrained?

65. When you are at a meeting and someone tells a joke, do you
  a) laugh and think of one to tell, or
  b) sit and listen more or less passively?

66. In a performance appraisal, would it be more accurate if your boss said
  a) you are practical, or
  b) you are imaginative?

67. Are you usually more interested in how your colleagues
   a)   think about problems, or
   b)   feel about problems?

68. When a new and unusual policy announcement is issued at work, are you usually
   a)   annoyed or otherwise upset at the changes, or
   b)   interested in seeing how you will handle the new environment?

69. In a meeting, do you usually
   a)   speak out directly when you want to, or
   b)   wait until you are asked directly before you speak?

70. When you start a new project, do you usually
   a)   write a step-by-step plan early in the process, or
   b)   wait and see how things develop before planning?

71. When you have a decision to make at work, do you usually
   a)   reason it through regardless of your feelings, or
   b)   consider your feelings to be very important?

72. If they couldn't be both, would you rather have colleagues who are
   a)   well organized, or
   b)   spontaneous?

73. Would you prefer to work in a company where
   a)   everyone works together in an open, active environment, or
   b)   people work independently in their own spaces?

74. Do you more often seek out work that applies your
   a)   practical skills and nature, or
   b)   your ability to create new ideas and things?

75. When you have to make a decision at work, are you more likely to
   a)   analyze the situation logically, or
   b)   put a strong emphasis on applying your values to the solution?

76. When you present your views in a meeting, are you usually
   a)   clear and decisive, or
   b)   open to having others suggest changes and other views?

77. When you need to pass on an idea or information, do you prefer to
   a)   talk directly to people about it, or
   b)   put it in writing?

78. Is your leadership style more
   a)   practical, or
   b)   visionary?

14

79. In a performance appraisal meeting, are you usually more likely to
   a)   be frank and honest regardless of feelings, or
   b)   try to smooth over any problems and avoid hurt feelings?

80. When you are discussing an important issue at a meeting, do you usually?
   a)   try to reach a definite conclusion quickly, or
   b)   keep the options open?

81. Do you enjoy more
   a)   a work day filled with variety and interactions with others, or
   b)   working without interacting with others for periods of time?

82. Do you prefer a work situation that is
   a)   stable with little change, or
   b)   full of change?

83. Would colleagues be more likely to describe your behavior at work as
   a)   cool, calm, and objective, or
   b)   warm and feeling?

84. At work, do you tend to
   a)   feel strongly about completing things on schedule, or
   b)   be flexible about changing deadlines?

85. When you are in a meeting with your colleagues and a high ranking employee comes in, do you usually
   a)   greet the person in a comfortable and friendly way, or
   b)   wait until you see how others react to him/her?

86. When you think of your most important work assets, are they
   a)   more in the realm of the practical, or
   b)   more inclined toward the realm of ideas?

87. In a training session or course, do you prefer a trainer who is
   a)   concise, logical, and to the point, or
   b)   genuine and touching?

88. Do you usually push your colleagues or subordinates for
   a)   quick decisions, or
   b)   thorough review, even at the risk of delaying decisions?

Scoring Your Work Type

On the Type Scoring Form on page 17, put a check (√) in the (a) or (b) box corresponding to your answer for each question. Add up the checks in each column. The larger score of each pair is the letter that indicates your type preference. Write the four letters in the spaces provided below:

My Type is: _____ _____ _____ _____

Now proceed to the pages following the scoring form for an explanation of the type preferences and a description of your style. When you have completed reading about your style, use your own words to summarize the material that describes your work type and style. Write only those portions of the description that you feel apply to you. Add any additional ideas, thoughts, or feelings that you have about your type and style. Write as much as you feel necessary to describe yourself fully and with satisfaction. See pages 99 to 112 in the Personal Career Profile chapter for examples of such a description.

Note: If you would like to learn more about your type, we suggest you take the Myers-Briggs Type Indicator® (a registered trademark of Consulting Psychologists Press, Inc.). The MBTI is a well researched and validated instrument which only trained, qualified individuals are allowed to purchase and administer. In order to find out where you can take the MBTI and have it interpreted, you may want to contact the following organizations that promote the understanding and ethical use of psychological type. These organizations will be able to provide you with MBTI resources in your area: *Association for Psychological Type (APT)*, P.O. Box 5099, Gainesville, FL 32609, (904) 371-1853; *Center for Applications of Psychological Type (CAPT)*, 2720 NW 6th Street, Gainesville, FL 32609, (904) 375-0160; Consulting Psychologists Press, 577 College Avenue, Palo Alto, CA 94306-1490, (415) 857-1444.

Summary:

	a	b		a	b		a	b		a	b
1			2			3			4		
5			6			7			8		
9			10			11			12		
13			14			15			16		
17			18			19			20		
21			22			23			24		
25			26			27			28		
29			30			31			32		
33			34			35			36		
37			38			39			40		
41			42			43			44		
45			46			47			48		
49			50			51			52		
53			54			55			56		
57			58			59			60		
61			62			63			64		
65			66			67			68		
69			70			71			72		
73			74			75			76		
77			78			79			80		
81			82			83			84		
85			86			87			88		

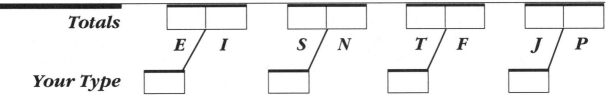

Totals

E / I S / N T / F J / P

Your Type

17

Work Type

*T*he four-letter type you just discovered represents a category of preferences that will help to define your style. Each type determines a different style or complex set of behavioral preferences. The notion of preferences and their effect on style was first discovered by the psychiatrist Carl Jung. In order to make Jung's work accessible to people and useful in self-understanding, Isabel Briggs Myers and Katharine C. Briggs devised an assessment of type called the Myers-Briggs Type Indicator® (a registered trademark of Consulting Psychologists Press, Inc.) (MBTI). They described four processes and attitudes to describe an individual's type.

1.   Extraversion-Introversion

This indicator refers to an individual's preference for extraversion (E) or introversion (I). Extraverts are primarily oriented toward activity and awareness in the external world and look more outside of themselves to interactions with other people to derive energy. Introverts are primarily oriented toward looking inward to the world of ideas, and tend to be most comfortable in the world of ideas and energized by their inner world.

2.   Perception

The second indicator refers to the two ways we have of perceiving the world and taking in information – sensing (S) through our five senses, or through intuition (N) which is the process of perceiving the world through meanings and relationships that we cannot see, hear, smell, taste, or feel. People who prefer sensing are more interested in what is actually in the environment around them, and tend to perceive the world in a more factual, concrete, and specific way. People who prefer intuition like to read between the lines and look for the possibilities in things rather than concentrate on the things themselves. They tend to take a more global, "big picture" view of things.

3.   Judgment

The third indicator refers to the two ways we have of reaching conclusions about what we have perceived – thinking (T) in which we reach conclusions based on logical, objective processes, or feeling (F) in which conclusions are made more subjectively and on the basis of personal values. The person who prefers thinking will judge things in the world on whether they are consistent and logical with the individual's ideas tested through reasoning. *A preference for judging by thinking does not mean that you are judgmental!* The person who prefers feeling is more likely to judge things in the world on the basis of whether they are pleasing or appealing or threatening or otherwise consistent with the individual's values. *A preference for judging by feeling does not refer to emotions or feelings!*

4.   Process for Dealing With the Outer World

The final indicator refers to the preferred process that an individual uses in relating to the outside world – judgment (J) in which the outer world is dealt with principally through one of the two judgment processes, thinking or feeling, or perception (P) in which the outside world is dealt with principally through one of the two perceiving processes, sensing or intuition. People who prefer the judging process like to bring things to completion in their lives. They prefer to approach life in a more organized and structured way. They prefer to make decisions and shut off the perceiving process to avoid adding confusion. Those who prefer the perceiving process like to keep things open and flowing, and tend to delay making decisions to allow time for further evidence to keep coming in. They prefer to approach life in a more open-ended, flexible, less structured manner.

Your Style

*T*here are 16 possible combinations of the four preferences. Each of these combinations represents a distinct work type with a style different in many characteristics from each of the others. When reading through these style descriptions, it is important to remember the following caveats:

1. No assessment of any kind is 100% accurate in predicting every behavioral characteristic or preference of an individual.

2. How you really perceive yourself is more important than what is predicted by theory. There is no such thing as a "pure type."

3. Do not necessarily rely completely on the assessment score to determine your type and its style. If the score for the two pairs in any of the dimensions was close and you are uncertain about which you really are, read the style descriptions for both of the types (e.g. if you are uncertain whether you are an ENTJ or an ESTJ because your S and N scores were close, read the descriptions for both ENTJ and ESTJ and see which you see, sense, think, or feel fits you better.)

4. No one type or style is better than any other – only different! The world needs every style, and a wide variety of styles can be found in almost every organization, family, team, or other collection of human beings. In addition, you use all of the functions and attitudes at different times. Your type only describes those you most prefer. Styles are complementary, and every group needs something from everyone. Extroverts need introverts, sensing types need intuitive types, thinkers need feelers, and people who process the world through their judgment need people around them who process the world through their perception.

Style Descriptions

*E*ach of the style descriptions presented on the following pages contains the following elements:

1. A brief statement characterizing the principal behavioral styles and preferences for the type.

2. A list of words associated with the specific type and style.

3. Preferred work environment.

4. Preferred interpersonal style.

5. Possible developmental needs.

The style descriptions are located on the following pages:

ISTJ

Analytical Manager of Facts and Details

Style:
ISTJ's are characterized as serious and quiet. They become successful through their ability to concentrate and perform tasks in a thorough manner. They are practical, logical, dependable, orderly, matter-of-fact, and well organized. They are not easily distracted and make up their own minds about how a job should be accomplished regardless of outside protest or interference. They pay great attention to details and operate well in stable environments. They do not like things that are frivolous or new, and are patient and sensible.

Words:
Conservative, decisive, dependable, duty bound, factual, organized, painstaking, practical, realistic, reliable, sensible, stable, steadfast, systematic, thorough.

Preferred Work Environment:
They prefer to work in a structured, orderly, task-oriented environment that allows them to work independently and privately so that their work can be uninterrupted. They like organizations in which they have a good measure of security that will provide rewards for their steady work. They like their colleagues to be as hard-working as they are and to be interested in producing results from an analysis of the facts.

Interpersonal Style:
These people readily accept responsibility and are well organized. When they serve in leading administrative positions, they produce a stabilizing influence and show good judgment and a memory for details. When their own needs have been firmly established, they are able to respect the needs of others.

Possible Developmental Needs:
These people sometimes need to develop a deeper understanding of others with whom they are in relationship. It is particularly valuable for them to learn to acknowledge others clearly. They may need to give more attention to organizing the way they deal with the outer world and avoid becoming too preoccupied with their inner life. Attempting new approaches can keep them from getting stuck in monotonous routine.

ISFJ

Sympathetic Manager of Facts and Details

Style:
These people live their lives in a style that is quiet, responsible, and conscientious, and also are characterized as friendly. They work hard to maintain their responsibility and to serve their friends and co-workers. They are thorough and work with great accuracy. They are patient in dealing with details and routine, and need time to master technical material. They are loyal and considerate of the feelings of others. Dedicated and service-oriented individuals, they are dependable, orderly, traditional and relate well to individual needs.

Words:
Conscientious, conservative, dependable, detailed, devoted, helpful, loyal, meticulous, orderly, organized, painstaking, patient, practical, protective, responsible, service-minded, stable, sympathetic, systematic, traditional.

Preferred Work Environment:
They like a calm, orderly, and quiet environment in which they have privacy to work efficiently. They prefer security and a clearly structured way of working. Preferred colleagues include people who are working diligently on well-structured tasks. They like to work in an environment that provides practical services to people.

Interpersonal Style:
These people relate well to people who are in need. They are characterized as loyal, supportive, considerate, sympathetic and helpful. They communicate with personal warmth, and work hard to keep their word in dealing with friends. They prefer to associate with modest, quiet people.

Possible Developmental Needs:
They may need to develop a more direct and assertive, as well as a more positive, and optimistic approach to the world. It may also be helpful to develop an understanding of their own true value. At the same time, they may need to learn to delegate more to others and not overwork themselves. They should be prepared to take the time required to master technical subjects when necessary.

INFJ

People-Oriented Innovator of Ideas

Style:
These people manage their success through perseverance, originality, and the motivation to do whatever is required. They put their full selves and best efforts into their work. They often can be counted on to innovate new ideas. Quietly forceful, conscientious, concerned for others, they are respected for their firm principles. Their intuition is strong and generates a good deal of inspiration, which is important to them. They are likely to be honored for their leadership which is evidenced by enrolling others in their ideas, rather than making demands.

Words:
Committed, compassionate, conceptual, concerned, creative, deep, determined, empathetic, forceful, holistic, idealistic, intense, loyal, persevering, reserved, sensitive, serious.

Preferred Work Environment:
These people prefer a warm, human-oriented environment that allows time for quiet contemplation. There is also a preference for a place with opportunities to demonstrate creativity. Colleagues are preferred who are harmonious and who are committed to improving the world for people and supporting their well-being.

Interpersonal Style:
Highly empathetic in their dealings with others, they tend to earn respect for maintaining firm principles. They usually have a strong, long-term inner circle of friends with whom they share their feelings only after developing deep trust. They get along well with people who are complex and remain alert to their emotions and personal interests. They use acknowledgment as a way of winning the support of others.

Possible Developmental Needs:
They may need to become more active in both giving and accepting constructive criticism, rather than seeking harmony above all. Ideas that conflict with their values should be reviewed for merit rather than dismissed out of hand. They need to consider a full range of facts, figures and problems and avoid a single-minded concentration on personal vision.

INTJ

Logical, Critical, Decisive Innovator of Ideas

Style:

Marked by original minds and relentless innovation in thought as well as action, they are particularly turned on by very difficult problems and their strong faith in their intuitive power make them unusually successful problem-solvers. Characterized as skeptical, critical, independent, determined, and stubborn, they have the most independent style of all of the types. They are skilled at building systems and products using logic and theory. INTJ's place a high value on the competence of both themselves and others and will drive others just as hard as they drive themselves.

Words:

Autonomous, critical, decisive, demanding, firm, global, independent, individualistic, inspirational, logical, original, private, serious, systems-oriented, theoretical, visionary.

Preferred Work Environment:

These people prefer autonomy in their work and want privacy for thoughtful contemplation. They also prefer opportunities for expressing their creativity. Efficiency is preferred along with colleagues who are intellectually stimulating, productive, effective, and interested in dealing with long-range issues consistent with their vision of the future.

Interpersonal Style:

These are the hard-driving, independent, individualistic people who remain determined and decisive regardless of external conditions or people. They are oblivious to criticism or indifference and are often characterized as unyielding.

Possible Developmental Needs:

They may need to do a more thoughtful analysis of their ideas and develop a more realistic view in order to bring projects to fruition. It might be helpful to be more open and less stubborn when others present ideas. They may need to realize that a project requires care and activity throughout its life cycle and not only through the creative stages. They may need to give more attention to how their behavior affects other people.

ISTP

Practical Analyzer

Style:
These people may be characterized as "cool onlookers." They are quiet and reserved, and observe and analyze life with a detached curiosity and unexpected flashes of original humor. They are logical and analytical and are not likely to be swayed by anything but a well reasoned argument based on solid facts. They are action-oriented, precise, and tireless, but will exert themselves no more than they need to because they do not like inefficiency. They show a strong interest in the inner workings of things and are likely to excel in the applied sciences and engineering. Socially, they may be shy with everyone except their closest relationships.

Words:
Adaptable, adventurous, analytical, applied, curious, expedient, factual, independent, logical, observant, practical, realistic, reflective, self-determined, spontaneous.

Preferred Work Environment:
These people prefer an action-oriented environment among people who are focused on solving immediate problems. They like to be free to operate independently without too many organizational constraints, rules, and regulations. Projects on which they can have hands-on participation are preferred.

Interpersonal Style:
Although they tend toward shyness, they are action-oriented and prefer to demonstrate their views by example. They prefer to communicate directly and tell the truth about how they see things. They are loyal and generous in their relationships.

Possible Developmental Needs:
They may need to understand the purpose for authority and reduce a tendency toward insubordination. It may be important to develop the habit of planning, goal-setting, and working with perseverance toward the achievement of well-defined targets. They may need to become more open to the feelings and needs of others.

ISFP

Observant, Loyal Helper

Style:
Characterized by a modest, retiring, and quietly friendly face to the world, these people do not display the warmth that exists abundantly inside. They shun disagreements, but stick to their values with passionate conviction. They usually do not care to lead and can be passionate followers. They are tolerant, flexible, open-minded, and adaptable, and seek simplicity and freedom. They digest experience deeply and stubbornly hold onto their inner loyalties. They do not think of dominating or impressing others, and value those who are willing to understand their goals and inner beliefs. They live well in the moment and take their time about getting things done.

Words:
Adaptable, caring, cooperative, empathetic, flexible, gentle, harmonious, loyal, modest, observant, patient, realistic, reflective, retiring, sensitive, spontaneous, trusting, understanding.

Preferred Work Environment:
These people like to be in a compatible, harmonious, people-oriented situation working with colleagues who are quietly going about their business courteously and with some pleasure. The environment should be attractive and allow for some flexibility and a private place to work.

Interpersonal Style:
These people are good team players who accept direction from leaders. They do not spend time judging others, and have little need to dominate. They work best with people who are in alignment with and understand their goals. They use praise and loyalty rather than criticism to persuade and motivate others.

Possible Developmental Needs:
It may be important for them to develop a more assertive approach to their work, develop a more skeptical attitude, and learn to analyze rather than accept. They may need to learn to take feedback without being overly sensitive, learn to appreciate their own accomplishments more, and give constructive criticism to others. They may need to take a broader view, become more future-oriented, curb their impulses, and organize their time and resources in advance.

INFP

Imaginative, Independent Helper

Style:
Enthusiastic and loyal people, but not outspoken about these characteristics except to close relationships. Their deepest feelings are seldom expressed; their inner tenderness is masked by a quiet reserve. INFP's care about learning, ideas, language, and independent projects of their own. Their main strength lies in their intuitive sense of what is possible in reaching beyond the obvious, known present. They work best when they believe strongly in what they are doing and sometimes undertake heavy responsibilities in these conditions. They can be characterized as flexible, tolerant, and open-minded.

Words:
Adaptable, committed, compassionate, creative, curious, deep, devoted, empathetic, gentle, imaginative, independent, inquisitive, loyal, reticent, virtuous.

Preferred Work Environment:
These people prefer to work with others who are committed to people-related values in a cooperative environment with minimum bureaucracy and with opportunities for stimulating intuition as well as quiet time for reflection.

Interpersonal Style:
These people carry deep-seated feelings for others and are often too busy to socialize. They seldom express their feelings outwardly, but remain loyal and devoted to people and causes. They often communicate feelings through writing rather than speaking. They work best alone without interruption.

Possible Developmental Needs:
They may need to develop skills for the realistic and detailed planning of projects. It may be important for them to develop a tough-minded posture along with the ability to say "no." They may sometimes have to reduce their sights to avoid a self-defeating attitude of perfectionism.

INTP

Inquisitive Analyzer

Style:
Intensely analytical and objectively critical, these people are hair-splitting logicians. Mainly interested in ideas and intensely curious, they have little liking for small-talk or parties. They are quiet and reserved, but can be counted on to discuss in detail any subject about which they have studied or thought deeply. They learn quickly and their intuition strengthens their insight, ingenuity, and intellectual curiosity. They have sharply defined interests, are persevering and thorough, and are unimpressed with authority.

Words:
Autonomous, cognitive, curious, detached, independent, inquisitive, logical, original, precise, reflective, reserved, self-determined, skeptical, speculative, theoretical.

Preferred Work Environment:
These people like an unstructured environment that fosters independence, offers privacy and the opportunity to do thoughtful, independent work among others working in the same way on difficult problems.

Interpersonal Style:
Sometimes characterized as quiet and reserved, these people rely heavily on their strong logical ability to relate to others. They enjoy conversation steeped in infinitesimal logic and importance, and cannot tolerate small-talk. They have difficulty expressing emotions and are difficult to get to know.

Possible Developmental Needs:
They may need to understand the needs of other people and communicate in a way that others can understand and appreciate what is being said. It may be important to spend more time on the practical details and follow-through required in some projects.

ESTP

Realistic Adapter in the World of Material Things

Style:
These are the matter-of-fact people. They rely on what they see, hear, and know directly. They are confident that they will find a solution for any problem once they understand all of the facts. They work best with real things that can be worked, handled, taken apart or put together. They have a strong and active curiosity about anything they can see, smell, touch, hear, or taste, especially when it is new. Excellent problem solvers, they use their ability to see the need of the moment and meet it; absorb, apply, and remember great numbers of facts; display a strong artistic judgment and taste; and handle tools and materials with excellence. They are resourceful and make good negotiators.

Words:
Activity-oriented, adaptable, alert, charming, easygoing, energetic, friendly, fun-loving, good-natured, observant, outgoing, persuasive, popular, pragmatic, quick, realistic, spontaneous, versatile.

Preferred Work Environment::
These people prefer a flexible, technical environment with a minimum of rules, and time to enjoy themselves in responding to the needs of the moment among people who value first-hand experience and want to work in an attractive place.

Interpersonal Style:
They are diplomatic negotiators and very aware of what others want and need. These people are fun to be around and are amusing and interesting. They take risks and tend to be adventurous in their relationships.

Possible Developmental Needs:
They may need to temper their spontaneous and sometimes reckless actions with some realistic planning, a sense of commitment to something worthwhile, and the use of their high energy toward a constructive end.

ESFP

**Realistic
Adapter in
Human
Relationships**

Style:
Easy, outgoing, friendly, and accepting, these people rely on their direct senses. They look for a satisfying solution instead of trying to impose one that should or must be right. They are infectious in their enjoyment of things and make life more fun for those around them. They are unprejudiced, open-minded, and tolerant of almost everyone, including themselves. They work best in situations requiring common sense and practical ability with people and things. They are generous and optimistic, like company and excitement, are actively curious about people, food, activities, or other things that are new to their senses. They are tactful and sympathetic and display a real interest in people. They are very good at handling human contacts. Their learning style depends heavily on first-hand experience rather than traditional methods of books and lectures.

Words:
Adaptable, cooperative, easygoing, enthusiastic, friendly, outgoing, playful, pleasant, realistic, sociable, sympathetic, tactful, talkative, tolerant, vivacious, witty.

Preferred Work Environment:
These people prize a lively, energetic, and action-oriented workplace. They want to be among people who are easygoing, reality-oriented, adaptable, people-oriented and harmonious.

Interpersonal Style:
These people are open-minded and very interested in others. They are fun to be with and are witty, playful, and good conversationalists. They are good at conflict resolution and deal effectively with difficult personal situations on-the-spot. Their human contacts are flowing, and they are usually liked by others.

Possible Developmental Needs:
They may need to look twice to be certain that they have not overlooked a problem hiding behind affability. They may need to develop a better balance between their leisure and work time. When making decisions, it may be important to consider logic and long-range vision and reduce the tendency toward impulsiveness.

ENFP

Warmly Enthusiastic Planner of Change

Style:
Warmly enthusiastic, high-spirited, ingenious, and imaginative, these people are able to do almost anything that interests them. They are quick with a solution to almost any difficulty and are ready to help anyone with a problem. They are enthusiastic innovators and see new ways of doing things, having considerable energy for carrying out projects that are generated by their imagination and initiative. Their use of feeling judgment also adds depth to the insights provided by their intuition. They are gifted observers and enterprisers and are charming and well liked.

Words:
Adaptive, creative, curious, energetic, enthusiastic, expressive, friendly, gentle, imaginative, independent, individualistic, inspirational, inventive, perceptive, restless, spontaneous, sympathetic, understanding, versatile, warm.

Preferred Work Environment:
These people prefer an environment with a minimum of constraints and a maximum of lively, imaginative colleagues working in a colorful, participative atmosphere concentrating on human potential.

Interpersonal Style:
These people are active in maintaining their relationships, keeping their options open, and doing everything they can to avoid conflict and disharmony. They usually have a large network of contacts and are skilled at understanding people. They are characterized as gentle, warm, and sympathetic to others and are good at presenting new insights into personal problems.

Possible Developmental Needs:
It may be important for them to develop an ability to manage their time and projects effectively, avoid moving on to new projects before the old ones are finished, and give more time to studying relevant details. They may need to become better organized, particularly when it comes to prioritizing their work.

ENTP

Inventive, Analytical Planner of Change

Style:
Characterized by a quick ingenuity, they are good at many things. They make stimulating company and are alert and outspoken. They are extremely perceptive about the attitudes of other people and use this knowledge to enroll others in supporting their endeavors. They are objective in their approach to projects and to the people in their lives. They move from one interest to another and are skillful in finding logical reasons for what they want. They like novelty and uncertainty, love challenges, and are pragmatic and goal-oriented. They enjoy feeling competent in a variety of areas and value this in others as well.

Words:
Adaptive, analytical, challenging, clever, creative, enterprising, enthusiastic, independent, individualistic, inspirational, inventive, outspoken, questioning, resourceful, strategic, theoretical.

Preferred Work Environment:
These people prefer an environment that encourages risk-taking and autonomy. They like to work among people who are independent and involved in complex problems in a flexible atmosphere with few bureaucratic constraints.

Interpersonal Style:
Although they tend toward the impersonal side, they can inspire others by their natural enthusiasm. They prefer to understand rather than judge people and deal imaginatively with their relationships. They are often more concerned about people's affect on their work than on how their work may affect others.

Possible Developmental Needs:
They may find it important to apply themselves to understanding and following through on the details of a project to ensure that the project is neither poorly selected nor unfinished. They may need to set realistic priorities, targets, and schedules, and acknowledge the contribution that others have to make.

ESTJ

Fact-minded, Practical Organizer

Style:
These people like to organize projects and make sure that they are completed. They tend to focus on the job that needs to get done, rather than on the people who need to do it. They are practical, realistic, matter-of-fact, with a natural head for business or mechanics. They have little interest in subjects for which they see no practical use. They are characterized as responsible, orderly, loyal and steadfast. They enjoy being involved in community activities. They are more interested in seeing present realities than future possibilities and use past experience and solid facts to help them solve problems. They like projects where the results of their work are immediate, visible, and tangible.

Words:
Aggressive, analytic, conscientious, decisive, direct, efficient, fact-minded, forceful, impersonal, logical, objective, organized, practical, responsible, serious, structured, systematic, thorough.

Preferred Work Environment:
These people prefer the hard-working, results-oriented and structured environment among people who are intensely focused on "getting the job done." They prefer structure and rewards for meeting goals.

Interpersonal Style:
These people are serious, forceful, and thorough and are less concerned with their emotional life than with practical considerations. They maintain consistency in their relationships, can be tough when they need to discipline others, and are easy to get to know and understand – little is hidden. They like to organize and run things.

Possible Developmental Needs:
It may be important for them to develop patience, a slower pace when dealing with others, and a more thoughtful consideration of facts and the human side before reaching conclusions. They may need to make a special effort to acknowledge the contribution of others.

ESFJ

Practical Harmonizer and Worker With People

Style:

Born cooperators, ESFJ's are warm-hearted, talkative, popular, conscientious and active committee members. They have an excellent gift for finding value in other people's opinions. They work best with encouragement and praise and are always doing something nice for someone. They are practical, realistic, and down-to-earth and enjoy their possessions. They are responsible, attentive, loyal, hardworking, and traditional. Much of their pleasure and satisfaction comes from the warmth of feeling of people around them. These people have little interest in abstract thinking or technical subjects, and their main interest is in things that directly and visibly affect people's lives.

Words:

Compassionate, conscientious, cooperative, friendly, harmonious, loyal, opinioned, orderly, outgoing, personable, popular, realistic, responsible, responsive, sociable, sympathetic, tactful, thorough, traditional.

Preferred Work Environment:

These people prefer a friendly, cooperative environment that is well organized with systems and an orientation toward achieving defined goals. They like to work with people who are sensitive, friendly, focused on helping others, and appreciative when they are served.

Interpersonal Style:

These people are recognized as popular, cooperative, and open to the opinions of others. They consider their relationships important and maintain them with energy and intelligence. They are open to the opinions of others, have their own strong opinions, and are sensitive to indifference or criticism.

Possible Developmental Needs:

It may be important for them to appreciate the value of a detailed and complex analysis of a problem when that is appropriate. They may need to understand the value of conflict and learn to accept it when it is needed. They may have to open their eyes to the facts in those situations that are disagreeable or discordant.

ENFJ

**Imaginative
Harmonizer
and Worker
With People**

Style:
These people generally feel real concern for what others think or want and try to handle things with due regard for other people's feelings. They can present a proposal or lead a group discussion with ease and tact. ENFJ's tend to concentrate on the best qualities of other people and maintain their loyalty to people they respect, and to institutions and causes, and sometimes admire things to the point of idealization. They think best when they are talking to people and are more likely to be gifted in their speaking expression rather than in writing. Natural leaders, they are social, popular, and active, but put considerable time into getting their jobs done. They can be characterized as tolerant, trustworthy, and forgiving.

Words:
Caring, concerned, congenial, conscientious, curious, diplomatic, energetic, enthusiastic, expressive, idealistic, loyal, nurturing, opinioned, orderly, personable, popular, responsible, sociable, supportive, verbal.

Preferred Work Environment:
These people prefer an orderly environment without too much change and the maximum opportunity for self-expression. They value a supportive workplace among people who operate with a spirit of harmony and are dedicated to changing the world for the benefit of humanity.

Interpersonal Style:
These people are nurturing and supportive and show an unusual amount of regard for others. They are popular and make good public speakers. They express their concern and responsibility for others and are seldom critical. They are usually considered gracious and socially adept.

Possible Developmental Needs:
They may need to develop an ability to manage conflict in a productive way. It may be important to set aside personal feelings and relationships when the facts warrant an objective look at a situation. They may need to recognize that people have limitations and that blind loyalty is not always appropriate.

ENTJ

**Intuitive,
Innovative
Organizer**

Style:

These people enjoy executive action and run as much of the world as they can get their hands on. They like to think ahead, organize plans, and make a systematic effort to reach their objectives on schedule. They seek leadership roles and express themselves in a hearty and frank way. They are able in their studies and work. They are usually well-informed and enjoy adding to their fund of knowledge. They are seldom content in jobs that make no demand on their intuition. They have a strong desire to give structure to things. They strive for efficiency and effectiveness and make a systematic effort to reach their objectives on schedule. They have little patience for confusion or inefficiency and can be tough when the situation calls for it.

Words:

Aggressive, analytical, challenging, controlled, critical, decisive, fair, innovative, intuitive, logical, objective, organized, straightforward, strategic, systematic, theoretical, tough.

Preferred Work Environment:

These people want to work among tough-minded and independent colleagues in a structured and challenging, goal-oriented environment that rewards firm decision-making.

Interpersonal Style:

These people have a strong need to lead others and drive them as hard as they drive themselves. They value logic and have little patience with confusion and inefficiency. They are critical and can be insensitive to the feelings of others.

Possible Developmental Needs:

They may need to be become highly conscious of the need to acknowledge others at appropriate times. It may be important for them to be more thorough in developing and understanding the facts before making decisions. They may need to avoid communicating confidence before experience really justifies it. They may need to bring more sensing types into their immediate environment.

*I*n addition to your work type, there is a way of describing your natural preferences in the world of work – your career type.

*C*areer type has to do with the relationship of our personality to the kinds *of work we like to do, the occupations we choose, and the work environments* in which we thrive.

Some career specialists have made direct connections between personality traits and career orientations. The most notable of these researchers is John Holland who introduced six personality/occupation types which we call here career types:

1. **(R)** Realistic
2. **(I)** Investigative
3. **(A)** Artistic

4. **(S)** Social
5. **(E)** Enterprising
6. **(C)** Conventional

Assessing Your Career Type

*W*hile there are various assessment instruments that can be used to indicate career type, it is informative and interesting to determine your career type by self-assessment. The process is simple.

On the following pages, each of the six career types is described in detail. The descriptions contain the following elements:

1. A brief statement characterizing the principal behavioral styles and preferences for the type.

2. A list of words associated with the specific type and style.

3. Preferred work environment.

4. Preferred interpersonal style.

5. Possible developmental needs.

6. Typical occupations and job titles.

Read through each of the six types and select the one you consider to provide the most accurate description of your own career type or style. In addition, select second and third career types that you feel provide some aspect of your own career type or style.

After you have determined your three top career types write them in the spaces below. Put the letter corresponding to each type in the parentheses. These three-letter types are also called Holland Codes, after John Holland who developed this typology, and reflect your overall occupational orientation.

Primary Career Type: (   )

Secondary Career Type: (   )

Tertiary Career Type: (   )

Now, use your own words to describe and summarize the material that describes your primary, secondary, and tertiary career types. Write only those portions that you feel apply to you. Add any additional ideas, thoughts, or feelings that you have about your types. Write as much as you feel necessary to describe yourself fully and with satisfaction. See pages 99 to 112 in the chapter on the *Personal Career Profile* for examples of such a description.

Summary:

*A*t the end of the first paragraph of the career types described on the following pages, the type of occupations toward which the career type tends to gravitate is discussed in broad terms. In the last paragraph is a list of the typical occupations and job titles associated with that career type. Read through these lists for your primary, secondary, and tertiary career type and write down any occupations or job titles that are of interest to you. Add any occupational groups or job titles that are of interest to you that may not be included on the lists.

Priority   **Career Interests**

[ ] _____

[ ] _____

[ ] _____

[ ] _____

[ ] _____

[ ] _____

[ ] _____

[ ] _____

[ ] _____

[ ] _____

[ ] _____

[ ] _____

[ ] _____

[ ] _____

[ ] _____

Write a 1 in the space to the left of the occupation or job title you consider to be the one of greatest interest to you, a 2 for the next most important, etc., until you have selected the five occupations or job titles of greatest interest to you.

Realistic

Style:
Typically, these are people who prefer to deal more with things than with ideas or people, are more oriented to the present than to the past or future, and have structured patterns of thought. They perceive themselves as having mechanical and athletic ability. They are apt to value concrete things or tangible personal characteristics like money, power, and status. They will try to avoid goals, values, and tasks which require subjectivity, intellectualism, or social skills. Realistic people prefer action to words and show impatience with those who prefer to talk about issues rather than do something about them. They prefer to produce useful things that are well made. They tend to be conservative in their attitudes and values because they have been tested and are reliable. Individuals of this type tend to be found in occupations related to engineering, skilled trades, agricultural, and technical vocations.

Words:
Aggressive, concrete, conservative, frank, hands-on, independent, persistent, physical, practical, rugged individualist, self-reliant, stable, strong, thrifty, traditional, well-coordinated.

Preferred Work Environment:
Realistic types prefer outdoor work, or working in laboratories, factories, or machine shops with their hands, where they can wear casual clothes and be with similar and familiar people. They like working in teams where the achievement of making something useful or getting a physical task completed is important. They prefer structured work environments.

Interpersonal Style:
They tend to be quiet and reserved without showing much emotion. They usually have a small group of very close friends with whom they spend most of their time and maintain these friendships over long periods of time. They may be wary of people who come into their environment who dress, look, or speak differently. They can be extremely loyal to people, organizations, and ideas that have traditional appeal.

Possible Developmental Needs:
It may be important for realistic types to develop stronger interpersonal communications. They may need to learn to give acknowledgment, listen to the needs of others, be more aggressive in seeking relationships with people who differ from them, and be more open in their acceptance of new ideas.

Typical Occupations and Job Titles:
Individuals of this type tend to be found in occupations related to engineering, skilled trades, agricultural, and technical vocations. Typical realistic job titles include, architect, athletic trainer, bus driver, carpenter, electrician, emergency medical technician, engineer, farmer, forester, horticulturist, military officer, physical education teacher, police officer, radiology technician, veterinarian, vocational teacher.

Investigative

Style:
These individuals are characterized as analytical, comfortable with abstractions and prefer to cope with life and its problems by the use of analytical thinking. They perceive themselves as scholarly, self-confident, and having mathematical and scientific ability. They hold conservative attitudes and values, tend to try to avoid close interpersonal relationships with groups or new individuals, and achieve primarily in academic and scientific areas. They are likely to possess a high degree of originality, as well as verbal and mathematical skills. Individuals with this orientation tend to be found in occupations related to science, math, social science professions, and other technical areas, including computer science, engineering, and the medical sciences.

Words:
Analytical, creative, curious, explorative, independent, inquisitive, intellectual, original, precise, rational, unconventional.

Preferred Work Environment:
Investigative types prefer to work in laboratories, libraries, universities, or other places where their inquisitive nature and interest in research and investigation can be well supported. They tend to work as individual contributors, although they can be effective team members when properly motivated and when left to perform independent work at appropriate times. They prefer to work with people who are achievement oriented and who value intelligence and logical thinking.

Interpersonal Style:
They usually prefer a strong, even argumentative, intellectual discussion about a topic of interest or expertise than any other kind of interaction. Investigative types can be withdrawn when they are deeply involved in a project or learning a new skill or concept. They can have faithful and long-term relationships, usually with a small number of close friends or colleagues. They gravitate toward people who match their lifestyle and intellectual interests.

Possible Developmental Needs:
They may need to develop stronger interpersonal skills, especially if they are involved in management. Assertiveness and leadership training, along with developing the ability to communicate abstract ideas clearly may be helpful. Some investigative types may also need training in organizing their work and in making decisions in a more timely and practical way.

Typical Occupations and Job Titles:
Individuals with this orientation tend to be found in occupations related to science, math, and other technical areas. Typical job titles include biologist, chemist, chiropractor, college professor, computer programmer, dentist, dietitian, geographer, geologist, mathematician, medical technician, nurse, optometrist, pharmacist, physical therapist, physician, physicist, psychologist, research & development manager, science teacher, sociologist, systems analyst, veterinarian.

41

Artistic

Style:
These are people who tend to rely especially on feelings and imagination in their work. They perceive themselves as expressive, original, intuitive, non-conforming, introspective, independent, and having artistic and musical ability (acting, writing, painting, sculpting, etc.). They find an important mode of communication through the expression of their creative abilities and tend to be idea oriented. Individuals with this orientation tend to be found in occupations related to music, literature, the fine arts, the dramatic arts, advertising, journalism, or a wide range of design fields including the design of programs and services, as well as other creative forms.

Words:
Creative, emotional, expressive, idealistic, imaginative, impulsive, independent, intuitive, non-conforming, original, spontaneous.

Preferred Work Environment:
Artistic people prefer unstructured, informal, private, quiet places where they can work alone or with a small group of people involved in a single project where they have considerable latitude for self-expression. They often work best unsupervised in an environment where they feel a sense of meaning in their work and where processes are more important than results and quality is more critical than quantity.

Interpersonal Style:
While they prefer to use the product of their work to express their feelings and thoughts, they are able to communicate with style and flair and express their ideas with emotion and strength. Artistic types prefer to be with people who are also involved in activities involving creative expression and the fashioning of artistic products.

Possible Developmental Needs:
It may be important for them to develop communication skills that use logic and organization. They may need to develop planning skills and practice working with others in an environment requiring cooperation. They may need to give more attention to caring about and respecting the ideas of others. They may also need to give more attention to details and gather more factual information.

Typical Occupations and Job Titles:
Artistic individuals tend to be found in occupations related to music, literature, the dramatic arts, and other creative and self-expressive fields. Typical job titles include actor, actress, advertising copywriter, architect, art teacher, author, ballet dancer, beautician, broadcaster, chef, cinematographer, commercial artist, film director, fine artist, illustrator, interior decorator, journalist, linguist, medical illustrator, musician, photographer, playwright, sculptor.

Social

Style:

Persons with a social orientation have high interest in other people and are sensitive to the needs of others. They perceive themselves as liking to help others, understanding others, having teaching abilities, and lacking mechanical and scientific aptitude. They value social activities, solving social problems, and interpersonal relations. They use their verbal and social skills to influence other people's behavior. They usually are cheerful and impulsive, scholarly, and verbally oriented. Individuals with this orientation tend to be in occupations related to teaching, health care, social welfare positions, service oriented industries and professions, and the helping vocations.

Words:

Concerned, cooperative, ethical, friendly, generous, genuine, helpful, humanistic, kind, perceptive, responsible, sensitive, sociable, supportive, tactful, understanding.

Preferred Work Environment:

Social types work well in a wide variety of environments. They prefer to work with others in the service of people or in forwarding ideas and activities that contribute to the world. They are good team members and prefer a congenial, harmonious environment of specific achievement.

Interpersonal Style:

These people are characterized as warm, friendly, open, and communicative. They may have a wide circle of friends and colleagues with whom they share a deep appreciation of the quality and value of diversity in people. They understand the feelings of others and may often serve as informal counselors to their friends.

Possible Developmental Needs:

Social types may need to develop more effective management and organizational skills including team building and leadership. It may be important for them to develop an appreciation for financial planning and the constraints involved in budgeting, as well as the importance of administrative efficiency and organization required to get things done. They may also need to develop assertiveness and conflict management skills and pay more attention to political realities.

Typical Occupations and Job Titles:

Individuals with this orientation tend to be in occupations related to teaching, social welfare, human resources and personnel work, the leisure industry (hotels, resorts, and other service-oriented environments) and the helping professions and vocations. Typical job titles include concierge, consumer advocate, environmental attorney, human resources generalist, guidance counselor, legal aid attorney, minister, nurse, occupational therapist, physician, psychologist, social worker, teacher, training & development specialist, travel agent.

Enterprising

Style:
Enterprising people tend to be adventurous, dominant, and persuasive. They place high value on political and economic matters and are drawn to power and leadership roles. They perceive themselves as aggressive, popular, self-confident, social, possessing leadership and speaking abilities and lacking scientific ability. They enjoy influencing people and use their social skills with others to obtain their political or economic goals. Individuals with this orientation tend to be found in occupations related to sales, marketing and management, or in the professions of law, politics, and consulting.

Words:
Adventuresome, aggressive, ambitious, assertive, competitive, confident, domineering, energetic, persuasive, political, sociable, status conscious, verbal.

Preferred Work Environment:
Enterprising people prefer to work in a hard-driving, well-organized, results-oriented environment where people are dedicated to achieving bottom-line results. They are leaders who are adept at organizing and leading people to produce a well-defined and valuable product or service for which they receive a high compensation.

Interpersonal Style:
Outgoing, strong communicators, enterprising people work hard at getting along with others particularly where it is important for them to achieve results. They may have a wide network of professional and personal relationships with whom they stay in active communication. They are energetic and may use their skills and other personal assets to benefit their community and the larger society around them.

Possible Developmental Needs:
They may need to develop greater empathy for others and learn to respect ideas that are not their own. It may be important to enhance their team building skills in the areas of personal communication, particularly acknowledgment, and the delivery of clear statements of expectations for results.

Typical Occupations and Job Titles:
Individuals with this orientation tend to be found in occupations related to sales, management or supervision of others, and leadership roles. Typical job titles include attorney, business executive, business manager, chef/owner, entrepreneur, florist, funeral director, life insurance agent, optician, political activist, public official, purchasing agent, realtor, restaurant manager, retail buyer, salesperson, store manager, travel agent/owner.

44

Conventional

Style:
Conventional individuals tend to be precise, organized, and work well in structured situations. They feel most comfortable with precise language and situations where accurate accounting is valued. They perceive themselves as conservative, orderly, and having administrative and information and data collection skills. They value business and economic achievement, material possessions, and status. Individuals with this orientation tend to be found in occupations related to financial services, business, computations, administration, office practice systems, and staff support advisory roles.

Words:
Accurate, careful, conforming, conscientious, conservative, efficient, orderly, organized, persevering, persistent, practical, precise, predictable, quiet, responsible, systematic.

Preferred Work Environment:
Conventional people prefer the structured, orderly environment of the office of an organized company with clear and well-defined rules and policies. They work well on teams when they have a clearly defined task that they can accomplish on their own and contribute back to the overall success of the team. They are loyal and hard-working subordinates when they are working for a leader who appreciates their contribution. When they work as managers they value efficiency and work in a structured, goal-oriented fashion. They value security and dislike ambiguous, fast-changing environments.

Interpersonal Style:
Often reserved, conventional people rely on their work to communicate for them. They make relationships slowly, resist change, and are likely to have a small group of long-term close friends with whom they share common experiences and life-style preferences.

Possible Developmental Needs:
They may need to develop more skill at expanding their modes of solving problems. It may also be important for them to learn techniques for handling change, making decisions under conditions of uncertainty, and being more assertive.

Typical Occupations and Job Titles:
Individuals with this orientation tend to be found in occupations related to accounting business, computations, and secretarial and clerical or administrative professions and vocations. Typical job titles include accountant, banker, business teacher, credit manager, dental assistant, dietitian, food service manager, housekeeping manager, IRS agent, math teacher, military enlisted personnel, nursing home administrator, office manager, secretary.

*T*he most important questions you need to ask yourself about your worklife deal with what you really want. *What is most important to me? What do I really care about? What are the attitudes and values and activities and people and environments that I most want in my worklife? What do I really want to do when I'm working?*

What Really Matters To You?

*I*n this section, you will inventory your motivations and begin to develop a pattern of what it is you really want out of work. You will make two specific assessments – your *Career Anchors* and your *Career Values and Needs*. In addition, since interests are a basic part of motivation, refer back to the *Career Interests* you selected in the chapter on *Career Type*. Together, these four factors – Interests, Values, Needs, and Career Anchors – along with your motivated skills, will give you comprehensive insight into what motivates you in your worklife.

Your Career Anchor

*I*n 1971, Edgar Schein of the Sloan School of Management at MIT observed that as an individual's career progresses, he or she develops a self-concept that embraces some explicit answers to the questions:

1. *What are my talents, skills, areas of competence? What are my strengths and what are my weaknesses?*

2. *What are my main motives, drives, goals in life? What am I after?*

3. *What are my values, the main criteria by which I judge what I am doing? Am I in the right kind of organization or job? How good do I feel about what I am doing?*

As we become more experienced in the world of work, our self-concept becomes more of an influence on our career choices.

The Career Anchor serves to define which of our needs has the highest priority; which of the factors in our worklives we may not be willing to give up because they represent who we really are. Many people are not really clear

47

about what is most important to them and find themselves making career choices that are inappropriate and lead to dissatisfaction at work. The purpose of knowing your Career Anchor is to develop sufficient insight to be able to make intelligent and appropriate career choices. Each of the anchors is discussed in detail following the assessment.

Assessing Your Career Anchor

*T*he items in this inventory are designed to help you identify the Career Anchor or self-concept that is most important to you in your worklife. As you answer the questions, think in terms of what it is you really want in your worklife. Reflect on the questions from the point of view of your ideal career or job – the one you would have if you had completely free choice with no constraints. You are attempting here to dig deep into what really matters to you. Remember, there are no right or wrong answers – only your answers.

For each statement, circle the number that best rates how important it is to you to have this factor in your worklife. How willing would you be to give it up? How critical is it for you to retain it?

		Very Important									Not Important
1.	To belong to an organization and have a secure, long-term position is…	10	9	8	7	6	5	4	3	2	1
2.	To have a strong sense of freedom and independence in my work is…	10	9	8	7	6	5	4	3	2	1
3.	To be able to work at the state-of-the-art is…	10	9	8	7	6	5	4	3	2	1
4.	To have a group of people that report to me is…	10	9	8	7	6	5	4	3	2	1
5.	To run my own business is…	10	9	8	7	6	5	4	3	2	1
6.	To dedicate my time to others is…	10	9	8	7	6	5	4	3	2	1
7.	To solve difficult problems of any kind is…	10	9	8	7	6	5	4	3	2	1
8.	To include my family in my worklife is…	10	9	8	7	6	5	4	3	2	1

		Very Important	*Not Important*

9. Good benefits, guaranteed work, and a retirement program are…   *10 9 8 7 6 5 4 3 2 1*

10. Being able to follow my own way without rigid rules imposed by an organization is…   *10 9 8 7 6 5 4 3 2 1*

11. Doing the work I was trained for and interested in rather than being promoted out of my field of interest is…   *10 9 8 7 6 5 4 3 2 1*

12. To have an influence on others is…   *10 9 8 7 6 5 4 3 2 1*

13. Building a new business is…   *10 9 8 7 6 5 4 3 2 1*

14. Being excited about a worthwhile cause is…   *10 9 8 7 6 5 4 3 2 1*

15. Having tough problems to solve is…   *10 9 8 7 6 5 4 3 2 1*

16. Integrating other parts of my life with my worklife is…   *10 9 8 7 6 5 4 3 2 1*

17. To have my work remain in the same location is…   *10 9 8 7 6 5 4 3 2 1*

18. To be able to choose my own work hours is…   *10 9 8 7 6 5 4 3 2 1*

19. Learning new technical skills is…   *10 9 8 7 6 5 4 3 2 1*

20. To work my way up the management ladder is…   *10 9 8 7 6 5 4 3 2 1*

21. To start from scratch and create something new and original is…   *10 9 8 7 6 5 4 3 2 1*

22. Being of service to others in a meaningful way is…   *10 9 8 7 6 5 4 3 2 1*

23. Reaching and growing beyond my current level is…   *10 9 8 7 6 5 4 3 2 1*

		Very Important									Not Important

24. Flexibility in location, work, and hours is...   *10 9 8 7 6 5 4 3 2 1*

25. Knowing where I will be working and what I will be doing year after year is...   *10 9 8 7 6 5 4 3 2 1*

26. The freedom to choose the direction of my career path is...   *10 9 8 7 6 5 4 3 2 1*

27. The ability to use technical skills or knowledge to complete a clearly defined project is...   *10 9 8 7 6 5 4 3 2 1*

28. Supervising, leading, and influencing others is...   *10 9 8 7 6 5 4 3 2 1*

29. Having the challenge of creating something new is...   *10 9 8 7 6 5 4 3 2 1*

30. Knowing that my work is contributing to the well-being of others is...   *10 9 8 7 6 5 4 3 2 1*

31. Having projects that stretch my abilities is...   *10 9 8 7 6 5 4 3 2 1*

32. Having sabbaticals or other leaves to pursue activities outside of work is...   *10 9 8 7 6 5 4 3 2 1*

How true is each of the following statements for you?

		Very True									Not True

33. I would be more interested in remaining in my present location rather than moving even if offered a promotion.   *10 9 8 7 6 5 4 3 2 1*

34. I am more concerned with my own freedom and autonomy than with any other factor in my worklife.   *10 9 8 7 6 5 4 3 2 1*

35. I am very proud of my technical and functional competence.   *10 9 8 7 6 5 4 3 2 1*

36. Managing other people gives me a strong sense of achievement.

10 9 8 7 6 5 4 3 2 1

37. Owning my own business is very important to me.

10 9 8 7 6 5 4 3 2 1

38. I am turned on by being dedicated to a worthwhile cause.

10 9 8 7 6 5 4 3 2 1

39. Projects are interesting to me only when they are really challenging.

10 9 8 7 6 5 4 3 2 1

40. I am more interested in an integrated lifestyle than in career promotion.

10 9 8 7 6 5 4 3 2 1

41. I need to belong to an organization to feel satisfied in my worklife.

10 9 8 7 6 5 4 3 2 1

42. The more freedom I have to do what I want the happier I am at work.

10 9 8 7 6 5 4 3 2 1

43. I would be interested in being a manager only if I could continue working in my area of expertise.

10 9 8 7 6 5 4 3 2 1

44. It gives me great satisfaction to be promoted into positions where I can exercise greater management authority.

10 9 8 7 6 5 4 3 2 1

45. Creating new business ideas and turning them into reality has been something I've wanted to do for a long time.

10 9 8 7 6 5 4 3 2 1

46. I enjoy volunteering with dedication to a cause even when there is little or no compensation.

10 9 8 7 6 5 4 3 2 1

47. I would live or work almost anywhere if the job had some real challenges.

10 9 8 7 6 5 4 3 2 1

48. My family, my hobbies, my friends, and my recreation are just as important to me as my work.

10 9 8 7 6 5 4 3 2 1

49. I would be unhappy working without job security.

10 9 8 7 6 5 4 3 2 1

50. I have difficulty dealing with organizational constraints.

10 9 8 7 6 5 4 3 2 1

51. Becoming more knowledgeable in my field is a great source of pride and satisfaction.

10 9 8 7 6 5 4 3 2 1

52. Supervising others and leading them to the achievement of targets and results is very important to me.

10 9 8 7 6 5 4 3 2 1

53. The thrill and tension of being on the edge in my own business is a strong motivator for me.

10 9 8 7 6 5 4 3 2 1

54. I think I have a contribution to make toward improving the world and helping people.

10 9 8 7 6 5 4 3 2 1

55. The challenge of competition turns me on to produce my best work.

10 9 8 7 6 5 4 3 2 1

56. I am only satisfied at work when my family life gets adequate attention.

10 9 8 7 6 5 4 3 2 1

57. I like being part of a large organization where I can be certain that my job, work, and salary are relatively secure.

10 9 8 7 6 5 4 3 2 1

58. I like working in a position that allows freedom and latitude.

10 9 8 7 6 5 4 3 2 1

59. I feel best when I can solve technical problems in my area of expertise.

10 9 8 7 6 5 4 3 2 1

60. I feel best when others come to me for advice about how to get their jobs done most effectively.

10 9 8 7 6 5 4 3 2 1

61. I want to own my own ideas, turn them into reality, and benefit from the money earned by creating something new.

10 9 8 7 6 5 4 3 2 1

62. I care more about people, the environment, peace and other critical issues than I do about promotions and success.

10 9 8 7 6 5 4 3 2 1

63. No pain no gain!

10 9 8 7 6 5 4 3 2 1

64. Happiness is a function of a balanced and integrated lifestyle.

10 9 8 7 6 5 4 3 2 1

Scoring Your Career Anchor

To find your Career Anchor, transfer your ratings on each of the 64 questions onto the scoring sheet on the following page. Add the scores down each column. The highest score is your Career Anchor. If any two scores are close (within 10 points), read the description of each of the two Career Anchors and see which you feel best describes your true preference. The Career Anchor indicated by your second highest score may also be an important indicator and should also be recorded. The Career Anchor descriptions follow the scoring form. Finally, if after reading through the descriptions you find that a particular Career Anchor is closer to your own self-perception than the one indicated by your score — use the one that you consider to be your own view of yourself!

After you have determined your Career Anchor, write it in the space provided below.

My Career Anchor is: _____

My Secondary Career Anchor is: _____

After you have read the descriptions, use your own words to describe and summarize the material that describes your primary and secondary Career Anchors. Write only those portions that you feel apply to you. Add any additional ideas, thoughts, or feelings that you have about your anchor. Write as much as you feel necessary to describe yourself fully and with satisfaction. See pages 99 to 112 in the chapter on *Personal Career Profile* for examples of such a description.

Summary:

[√] *Career Anchor Scoring Form*

Scoring

1	2	3	4	5	6	7	8
9	10	11	12	13	14	15	16
17	18	19	20	21	22	23	24
25	26	27	28	29	30	31	32
33	34	35	36	37	38	39	40
41	42	43	44	45	46	47	48
49	50	51	52	53	54	55	56
57	58	59	60	61	62	63	64

Totals

Security, Stability, Organizational Identity	Autonomy/Independence	Technical/Functional Competence	Managerial Competence	Entrepreneurial Creativity	Sense of Service/ Dedication to a Cause	Pure Challenge	Life-Style Integration

55

Descriptions of the Career Anchors

*O*ut of the many descriptions of self-concept that can be conceived, eight descriptioms appear to cover the full range and are identified as Career Anchors:

1. Security/Stability/Organizational Identity

2. Autonomy/Independence

3. Technical/Functional Competence

4. Managerial Competence

5. Entrepreneurial Creativity

6. Sense of Service/Dedication to a Cause

7. Pure Challenge

8. Life-Style Integration

Each of these eight career anchors is described on the following pages. For more detailed descriptions of the Career Anchors and for a copy of the original inventory developed by Schein, contact University Associates, Inc., 8517 Production Avenue, San Diego, CA 92121, (619) 578-5900.

Security, Stability, Organizational Identity

*T*his Career Anchor is usually subdivided into two categories. First, there are those people whose careers are anchored in the stability of employment in an organization. This person becomes strongly identified with the company and seeks the security of a long-term employment relationship, regular wages, and a modest progression through the ranks. They show loyalty, the willingness to change locations if the company and the job require it, and the acceptance of whatever assignments come along.

The second type of security anchor is geographic location. These individuals are strongly rooted in the region, often have most of their family resident in the same area, are active in the community, and may sacrifice promotion and standard of living to avoid moving from one location to another.

Success for security anchored people is experienced through having contributed to a company over the long haul, regardless of the level of that contribution.

Autonomy/Independence

*T*his anchor applies to people who have an overriding need to do things their own way, in their own time, and independent of others to the greatest extent possible. Being autonomous should not be confused with being an entrepreneur. Building a new business and taking risks is not necessarily a component of autonomy. People who value autonomy and independence may find the typical organizational roles constraining and prefer to pursue organizational career paths that are out of the ordinary. This independence is characteristic of what many organizations call individual contributors, or internal consultants.

The autonomy-anchored person does not feel a strong sense of loyalty or obligation to the organization and would probably refuse a promotion or transfer if it meant giving up independence. If they work in large organizations, they are attracted to jobs in which independence is possible such as research and development, field sales, data processing, financial analysis, etc.

Sometimes autonomous individuals reach a high level of education in their striving to be free, independent, and self-reliant. Many professionals such as university professors, doctors, lawyers, individual corporate contributors, internal corporate consultants, and free-lance consultants have chosen careers that allow them to express their autonomy.

Technical/Functional Competence

*T*he person anchored in technical or functional competence is most motivated towards being very knowledgeable and producing highly effective work in some field of specialization. They are primarily motivated by the content of the work they perform. These people tend to identify strongly with their expertise, and their self-concept is dependent on their ability to succeed and be recognized in their area of specialty.

Technical or functional competence may lead to a managerial position, but these people are only satisfied if they can manage within their discipline and would avoid a promotion if it meant leaving their specialty and losing their connection with that field. People with this anchor are seldom satisfied in a generalist position.

Every occupation and organization has its technical/functional specialists who are capable of making outstanding contributions when they are allowed to develop and use their expertise.

Managerial Competence

*T*he key motivations for people anchored in managerial competence are advancement up the corporate ladder to higher levels of responsibility, growing opportunities to serve in positions of leadership, increasing contribution to the overall success of the organization, and a long-term opportunity for high income and estate-building.

People committed to managerial competence recognize the need to excel in three basic areas of management – analytical, interpersonal, and emotional. *Analytical competence* is the ability to identify, analyze, and solve problems under conditions of uncertainty or incomplete information. *Interpersonal competence* includes the ability to supervise people and to influence, lead, and control them toward their achievement of organizational goals. *Emotional competence* includes the capacity to remain energized and proactive, without excessive anxiety or guilt, during periods of high stress, emotional and interpersonal crises, appearances of failure, and increasingly higher levels of responsibility and authority, and in general be able to handle the characteristic pressures and stresses that accompany management responsibilities.

The person with managerial competence as a Career Anchor has significant competence in all three areas, as differentiated from the technical or functional person who is highly developed in one skill area. This competence is recognized principally through promotion, and the managerial-anchored individual requires frequent promotions to remain satisfied.

Entrepreneurial Creativity

*T*he individual with an entrepreneurial anchor has a strong need to create a new business, the motivation to overcome obstacles, the willingness and the courage to run risks, and the desire for personal gain and recognition for what is accomplished.

It is important to separate entrepreneurial creativity from the autonomy anchor and from the technical/functional anchor. The entrepreneur is firmly rooted in ownership, creating a marketable and profitable product or service (regardless of the technology or intellectual discipline involved), and in making large amounts of money.

These individuals seldom stay with an organization that is not their own for long periods of time. They are eager to be fully active in an enterprise of their own creation where they can sink or swim on the merits of their personal ideas, abilities, personality, and drive.

Sense of Service/ Dedication to a Cause

*P*eople with a service anchor are characterized as being principally motivated by dedicating their work and sometimes their lives in the service of others. This dedication may take the form of working in a position in which they can directly serve others as counselors, physicians, therapists, nurses, or in the other helping and supportive occupations and professions. Service may also take the form of providing comfort, entertainment, leisure activities, athletic training, personal or business support activities (personal or administrative assistant), or any support service that represents a contribution to others.

They may also manifest this dedication through a commitment to the preservation or realization of a set of values that they consider important not only in their own lives but also in the larger world around them. Money is not usually an important motivator for these people. Recognition, along with financial and working support for their work and cause, is far more important and often drives their major activities – public relations, fund raising, and enrolling volunteers.

Not everyone with this anchor is dedicated to a charitable cause. For example, a scientist who has a desire to improve the environment may stay in a job only if he or she can work on environmental matters. A personnel manager may be expressing a desire to serve people. An executive assistant may be committed to serving his or her boss, and full-time parenting may be an expression of the service anchor.

Pure Challenge

*F*or the challenge-anchored person, the one thing that matters is being challenged at the highest possible level. Success is defined in terms of winning the war or the game or the contract or the sale, overcoming obstacles, being the best, being first, beating the competition, reaching for their highest, surpassing previous goals, and so on.

This person sees the area of work or the specific job to be performed as secondary to the experience of challenge. They often seek variety in their careers (and lives in general) and, in the absence of challenge, become highly dissatisfied. Easy things are boring.

Life-Style Integration

*F*or people whose anchor is life-style integration, work is not the major vehicle of self-expression. They are more interested in ensuring that they have a life balanced among various interests such as family, friends, hobbies, recreational and leisure activities, study and learning other than work-related subjects, and so on. They develop their self-concepts around issues of their total life styles, and how they define those life styles is the major guide and constraint on their careers.

These people choose jobs, careers, and organizations that allow them to make all the major sectors of their lives work together into an integrated whole. Career decisions do not dominate their lives.

Your Career Values and Needs

*T*his next exploration of your motivation will deal with your values and needs. Howard Figler, in *The Complete Job-Search Handbook*, defines work values as "...those enduring dimensions or aspects of our work that we regard as important sources of satisfaction."

Some values we hold strongly, others less so, and there is a scale along which we can measure our values. In the Career Values assessment that follows, you will examine your work values and determine how strongly you value each of them. This exercise will give you further insight into what motivates you in your worklife. This type of assessment is sometimes called "values clarification."

Needs are defined in the dictionary as *"a pressing lack of something essential"*, and thus take on a somewhat stronger sense of urgency than do values. Often, our values are reflections of underlying needs. It is often difficult to distinguish between those elements of experience that we value and those that we *need*. For example, Henry A. Murray described a model of manifest needs that includes *Achievement, Affiliation, Aggression, Autonomy, Exhibition, Harm Avoidance, Nurturance, Order, Power, Succorance, Understanding* and others. Some of these needs, including autonomy, achievement, order, and affiliation, can also be found on almost any list of career values. Therefore, the assessment provided here includes both needs and values in a single instrument. The assessment deals with what is really important to you, whether you experience them as needs or as values.

Assessing Your Career Values and Needs

*T*he items in this inventory are designed to help you identify the career values and needs that are most important to you in your worklife. As you answer the questions, think in terms of what it is you really value or need in your worklife. You are attempting here to dig deep into what really matters to you. Remember, there are no right or wrong answers – only your answers.

For each of the values and needs listed, check (√) whether it is Important, Neutral, or Unimportant to your worklife satisfaction.

		Important	Neutral	Unimportant
1.	**Achievement** Have the opportunity to excel and produce significant results, setting high standards for myself and doing work that is challenging.	[ ]	[ ]	[ ]
2.	**Advancement** Have my work lead to better opportunities for greater responsibility.	[ ]	[ ]	[ ]
3.	**Adventure/Excitement** Have work in which I am frequently excited about the activities or results, and take some risks.	[ ]	[ ]	[ ]
4.	**Aesthetics** Be involved in work that deals with creating or studying beautiful things.	[ ]	[ ]	[ ]
5.	**Affiliation** Identify myself and be recognized as belonging to a specific company or organization where I can develop close personal relationships or friendships.	[ ]	[ ]	[ ]
6.	**Artistic Creativity** Create objects, images, or other products of my own work in an art form.	[ ]	[ ]	[ ]
7.	**Attractive Environment** Work in an environment that I find attractive and comfortable to be in.	[ ]	[ ]	[ ]
8.	**Challenging Problems** Work frequently on issues and problems that will challenge my ability.	[ ]	[ ]	[ ]
9.	**Change and Variety** Have work that frequently is different in form, content, or location.	[ ]	[ ]	[ ]

10. Close to Power   [ ]   [ ]   [ ]
Have a position where I am in touch with the seats of power, where I have direct and frequent contact with influential people, where I am a part of big decisions.

11. Community   [ ]   [ ]   [ ]
Be involved in the affairs of the community in which I live.

12. Competition   [ ]   [ ]   [ ]
Work at jobs where I can test my abilities to win over others.

13. Control My Worklife   [ ]   [ ]   [ ]
Be in a position where I am in as much control of my workday as possible.

14. Creative Expression   [ ]   [ ]   [ ]
Create new concepts, products, services, structures, systems, etc. that do not follow established rules, procedures, and patterns.

15. Ethics   [ ]   [ ]   [ ]
Perform activities and work in an environment consistent with my moral principles and which do not violate my personal beliefs.

16. Exercise Competence   [ ]   [ ]   [ ]
Demonstrate that I do excellent work, understand my job well, and am considered a competent and effective person.

17. External Structure   [ ]   [ ]   [ ]
Work in an environment which provides structure in the form of broad guidelines to follow, objectives to achieve, and clear expectations. Have clear parameters under which to operate.

18. Exhibition   [ ]   [ ]   [ ]
Have an audience or group of people who are willing to listen to me where I can be the center of attention and win the notice of others.

19. Fame   [ ]   [ ]   [ ]
Be well known to a very large number of people for the quality of the work I do.

20. Fast Pace   [ ]   [ ]   [ ]
Work in an environment where results need to be produced quickly and on schedule.

62

21. **Field of Strong Interest**   [ ]   [ ]   [ ]
    Work in a field of major interest to me where I can perform activities
    of intrinsic interest.

22. **Help Society**   [ ]   [ ]   [ ]
    Work in a way that the benefits of my activities are widely spread
    throughout society.

23. **High Earnings**   [ ]   [ ]   [ ]
    Have an income that provides me with a high level of discretionary
    funds.

24. **Independence and Autonomy**   [ ]   [ ]   [ ]
    Be able to work without being told what to do or having to report
    back frequently.

25. **Influence People**   [ ]   [ ]   [ ]
    Have a position in which I have an affect on how people think.

26. **Intellectual Status**   [ ]   [ ]   [ ]
    Have others look at me as a person with high intelligence or as an
    expert in a specific field.

27. **Job Tranquility**   [ ]   [ ]   [ ]
    Work in an environment relatively free of stress and pressure.

28. **Knowledge**   [ ]   [ ]   [ ]
    Work in the pursuit of increased learning, professional development,
    and understanding in my field of expertise.

29. **Leadership**   [ ]   [ ]   [ ]
    Being the person to whom others look for vision and direction.

30. **Leisure**   [ ]   [ ]   [ ]
    Work in a position that enables me to have enough time to pursue
    activities of importance to me outside of work.

31. **Location**   [ ]   [ ]   [ ]
    Live in a place that allows me to express my life-style fully and easily,
    and provides easy access to my place of work.

32. **Make Decisions**   [ ]   [ ]   [ ]
    Be in a position to make decisions that affect the quality and success of
    outcomes.

33. Nurturing and Helping Others   [ ]   [ ]   [ ]

Have work that allows me to be supportive and understanding of others. To be involved in teaching, helping, guiding, curing, or providing a direct service to others.

34. Order   [ ]   [ ]   [ ]

Keep personal effects, surroundings, and work structures neat and organized, and work in an environment where things are done in a planned, systematic and orderly manner.

35. Physical Challenge   [ ]   [ ]   [ ]

Have a physically demanding and rewarding job.

36. Play   [ ]   [ ]   [ ]

Do things "just for fun" and spend time participating in games, sports, and other social activities and amusements. Maintain a light-hearted, easy-going attitude toward life.

37. Power and Authority   [ ]   [ ]   [ ]

Be in a position to control the work and the organizational future of others.

38. Precision Work   [ ]   [ ]   [ ]

Perform work in which fine tolerances are important and avoiding errors is critical.

39. Prestige/Recognition   [ ]   [ ]   [ ]

Do work that others consider to be important and to be recognized for the quality of my work.

40. Profit, Gain   [ ]   [ ]   [ ]

Have my work exercise a strong influence on the bottom line.

41. Public Contact   [ ]   [ ]   [ ]

Work face-to-face with the public.

42. Respect From Others   [ ]   [ ]   [ ]

Have others look on my ability with respect.

43. Security   [ ]   [ ]   [ ]

Know that I will keep my job and continue to receive reasonable compensation.

44. Stability   [ ]   [ ]   [ ]

Do work that changes little over long periods of time and is predictable.

45. *Status* [ ]   [ ]   [ ]
Have friends, family, and the community look at me with respect for my position.

46. *Supportive Environment/*
Supportive Supervisor [ ]   [ ]   [ ]
Work for a receptive boss/employer to whom I can comfortably turn for advice, counsel, help, and support.

47. *Time Freedom* [ ]   [ ]   [ ]
Keep my own schedule and be able to work at my own pace without pressure from others.

48. *Work Alone* [ ]   [ ]   [ ]
Produce results with little or no contact or input from others.

49. *Work on Frontiers of Knowledge* [ ]   [ ]   [ ]
Create new knowledge in the world about technical, social science, political science or other general, business, academic, or scientific subjects.

50. *Work Under Pressure* [ ]   [ ]   [ ]
Work in situations demanding high concentration under time pressure over long periods of time with little margin for error.

51. *Work With Others* [ ]   [ ]   [ ]
Work with other people toward common goals in a cooperative team effort.

Add any values or needs that may not have been included on the list that you feel are important to you.

52. _____

53. _____

54. _____

55. _____

56. _____

57. _____

58. _____

In the spaces provided below, list those values and needs which you checked as Important plus those that you added. For each value or need that you write below, decide whether you consider that your current worklife satisfies that value or need, or that it is not yet satisfied. Where you feel that one or more needs or values overlap in their meaning for you, either pick the one that best expresses that need or value for you, or put a multiple listing on the line.

Value Or Need

	Currently Satisfied	Not Yet Satisfied
1.	[ ]	[ ]
2.	[ ]	[ ]
3.	[ ]	[ ]
4.	[ ]	[ ]
5.	[ ]	[ ]
6.	[ ]	[ ]
7.	[ ]	[ ]
8.	[ ]	[ ]
9.	[ ]	[ ]
10.	[ ]	[ ]
11.	[ ]	[ ]
12.	[ ]	[ ]
13.	[ ]	[ ]
14.	[ ]	[ ]

Value Or Need

15._____ [ ]   [ ]

16._____ [ ]   [ ]

17._____ [ ]   [ ]

18._____ [ ]   [ ]

19._____ [ ]   [ ]

20._____ [ ]   [ ]

21._____ [ ]   [ ]

22._____ [ ]   [ ]

23._____ [ ]   [ ]

24._____ [ ]   [ ]

25._____ [ ]   [ ]

26._____ [ ]   [ ]

27._____ [ ]   [ ]

28._____ [ ]   [ ]

29._____ [ ]   [ ]

30._____ [ ]   [ ]

31._____ [ ]   [ ]

32._____ [ ]   [ ]

33._____ [ ]   [ ]

[√] *Most Important Values and Needs Currently Satisfied*

*F*rom the list you developed above, select up to 15 values and needs that you consider to be the most important to have in your worklife to insure your satisfaction and/or success, and which <u>are</u> currently satisfied in your worklife, and write them in the spaces provided below. Where you feel that one or more needs or values overlap in their meaning for you, either pick the one that best expresses that need or value for you, or put a multiple listing on the line. Use up to 15 lines.

Priority   **Values and Needs**

[ ] _____

[ ] _____

[ ] _____

[ ] _____

[ ] _____

[ ] _____

[ ] _____

[ ] _____

[ ] _____

[ ] _____

[ ] _____

[ ] _____

[ ] _____

[ ] _____

[ ] _____

Write a 1 in the box to the left of the value or need you consider to be your highest priority, a 2 for the next most important value or need, etc., until you have selected five (5) values or needs you consider most important to you.

[√] *Most Important Values and Needs Not Yet Satisfied*

From the list you developed above, select up to 15 values and needs that you consider to be the most important to have in your worklife to ensure your satisfaction and/or success, and which <u>are not yet</u> satisfied in your worklife, and write them in the spaces provided below. Where you feel that one or more needs or values overlap in their meaning for you, either pick the one that best expresses that need or value for you, or put a multiple listing on the line. Use up to 15 lines.

Priority   Values and Needs

[ ] _____

[ ] _____

[ ] _____

[ ] _____

[ ] _____

[ ] _____

[ ] _____

[ ] _____

[ ] _____

[ ] _____

[ ] _____

[ ] _____

[ ] _____

[ ] _____

[ ] _____

Write a 1 in the box to the left of the value or need you consider to be your highest priority, a 2 for the next most important value or need, etc., until you have selected five (5) values or needs you consider most important to you that are not yet satisfied.

*P*eople possess a wide variety of characteristics including a set of abilities that allow them to get things done in the world. Many people are not really aware of the full range of skills they possess. Their perception of what constitutes a skill is often limited to those technical skills learned in school or on the job.

You Are Not Your Job Title

*T*hey tend to identify themselves with their job title and those skills involved in getting their immediate jobs done. All of the other skills that people have are often taken for granted. The following structured process will allow you to discover the broad spectrum of skills with which you function in the world and discover those that are most important to your satisfaction, well-being, and success.

What Is a Skill?

*T*he dictionary provides us with six different ways of looking at the meaning of skill or skilled:

1. *Natural or acquired proficiency especially in a particular activity.*

2. *The quality or state of being ready or skillful.*

3. *A usually acquired proficiency in doing or performing.*

4. *The capacity to produce results with a minimum expenditure of energy, time, or resources.*

5. *A special method of doing, using, dealing with someone.*

6. *Proficiency and grace in dealing with others.*

Your skills are what you use to get things done, to accomplish your goals, to achieve your purposes. It is very important to remember that skills can be improved with practice and development. There are many resources available for those who want to improve their skills and effectiveness. See Chapter 9 for references that you can use to support your development.

Classification of Skills

People, Data, and Thing Skills
Wherever and whenever we work, and whatever we are doing when we work, we are always interacting and dealing with some combination of people, data, and things.

People Skills deal with our interactions with people including all forms of interpersonal communication, and a multitude of activities such as supervision, management, counseling, motivation, entertainment, teaching, serving, negotiating, persuading, and every other form of relating to other people.

Data Skills include every form of taking in, giving out, and manipulating any kind of information about people, data, and things. The information may be in the form of ideas, facts, figures, emotions, or other qualifiable or quantifiable factors. Anything that cannot be classified as a person or an object can be included in the category of data. Data activities include any form of analyzing, interpreting, judging, and sending and receiving of any kind of information. Information can be numbers, facts, sights, colors, sounds, or anything our minds and senses can experience.

Thing Skills have to do with the physical manipulation of real objects. Repairing, lifting, moving, making, typing, building, carrying, sawing, cutting, carving, filing, driving, handling, and holding are among the many thing activities. Dancing, walking, and running are included as thing activities because the real physical object being manipulated is your own body.

Most of the activities we do, and hence the skills we have, are combinations of people, data, and things. For example, when we write a letter on a word processor or typewriter or by hand to someone describing some fact or situation, we are combining a people activity (communicating), a thing activity (typing), and a data activity (describing information).

Notice if you consider yourself to be primarily a "people-person," "data-person," or "thing-person," and which of the other two is secondary and which is tertiary.

Functional, Adaptive, and Specific Content Skills
A secondary classification breaks skills down into three additional categories.

Functional Skills are those skills with which we deal with people, data, or things. Examples include – organize information logically, communicate clearly, write with style, lift heavy objects, analyze and solve problems, make decisions, and relate effectively to people.

Adaptive Skills (sometimes called *Self-Management Skills* or *Personal Qualities and Characteristics*) are those qualities that are temperament based and that we learn as we grow up in the world and need to or choose to use in order to fit (or adapt) ourselves into a variety of environments starting with our homes, school, and friends, and extending into the world of work. Poor adaptive skills is the reason most often cited by employers for firing someone. Many personality traits and characteristics can be thought of as skills or aptitudes because they enable us to get things done! Often, your overall personality may be your greatest aptitude. Examples include – persistence, confidence, thoroughness, patience, sensitivity, assertiveness, time management, and flexibility.

Specific Content Skills are knowledge-based and the ones used only in a particular job with little or no transferability to other kinds of work. Examples include knowing how to – operate a specific mainframe computer, operate a tower crane, perform open-heart surgery, assemble microcircuit boards, knowledge of tax law and how to make out a tax return, knowledge of a specific computer language, and how to grow orchids.

The importance of adaptive and functional skills is that they are transferable. That is, we can take them with us from any job or career to almost any other.

Motivated Skills

A final category of skills, and the most important for us as individuals, includes those specific content, adaptive, functional, people, data, and thing skills that we are motivated to include and use in our worklives. The motivation comes because we enjoy using those skills. Worklife satisfaction is obviously increased when we are in work situations that enable us to use our motivated skills – the skills we most enjoy using. Not using their motivated skills is a major source of job dissatisfaction for many people. Making use of these skills in our worklives is energizing and allows us to be more effective at work, as well as being more satisfied.

Assessing Your Motivated Functional Skills

Read through the following skill lists and for those skills that you prefer to use in your worklife (your motivated skills) check whether your current level of ability in that skill is acceptable or needs development.

By "acceptable" we mean that you consider yourself to be **reasonably effective**. You consider yourself to be a person who can use this skill **reasonably well.** Give yourself the benefit of the doubt and make sure not to think in terms of all or nothing, or make excessive, perfectionistic demands on yourself as you rate your skills.

By "needs development," we refer to those skills at which you consider yourself to be less than reasonably effective and that you would consider it personally important to work on and improve to enhance your effectiveness at work. Space is also provided for you to add skills that may not be included on these lists.

When you read through the skills, think — "I like to or would like to..." and complete the sentence with the appropriate skills from the lists.

[√] *Functional People Skills*

***Remember, check only those skills that you
are motivated to use in your worklife.***

Acceptable	Needs Development	"I like to or would like to…"	Acceptable	Needs Development	
[ ]	[ ]	Acknowledge others	[ ]	[ ]	Mediate
[ ]	[ ]	Act as liaison	[ ]	[ ]	Motivate others
[ ]	[ ]	Act as mentor	[ ]	[ ]	Negotiate contracts and agreements
[ ]	[ ]	Act assertively			
[ ]	[ ]	Appraise and develop others	[ ]	[ ]	Negotiate prices
[ ]	[ ]	Assist others to make decisions and solve problems	[ ]	[ ]	Network
			[ ]	[ ]	Persuade others
[ ]	[ ]	Build teams	[ ]	[ ]	Plan social occasions and activities
[ ]	[ ]	Coach			
[ ]	[ ]	Communicate clearly	[ ]	[ ]	Promote ideas
[ ]	[ ]	Communicate effectively	[ ]	[ ]	Provide others with information
[ ]	[ ]	Consult			
[ ]	[ ]	Coordinate people for effective performance	[ ]	[ ]	Relate to a wide variety of people
[ ]	[ ]	Counsel and advise people	[ ]	[ ]	Resolve conflict
[ ]	[ ]	Criticize constructively	[ ]	[ ]	Select people for positions
[ ]	[ ]	Delegate	[ ]	[ ]	Sell products
[ ]	[ ]	Develop good relationships	[ ]	[ ]	Sell services
[ ]	[ ]	Develop potential in others	[ ]	[ ]	Serve customers
[ ]	[ ]	Develop rapport with others	[ ]	[ ]	Serve others
[ ]	[ ]	Entertain	[ ]	[ ]	Settle disputes
[ ]	[ ]	Evaluate performance of others	[ ]	[ ]	Show warmth and support
			[ ]	[ ]	Speak well in public
[ ]	[ ]	Express feelings	[ ]	[ ]	Supervise
[ ]	[ ]	Express ideas	[ ]	[ ]	Teach
[ ]	[ ]	Facilitate groups	[ ]	[ ]	Train people
[ ]	[ ]	Follow instructions	[ ]	[ ]	Tune in to needs and feelings of others
[ ]	[ ]	Have empathy			
[ ]	[ ]	Heal people	[ ]	[ ]	Understand behavior
[ ]	[ ]	Help others	[ ]	[ ]	Work effectively on a team
[ ]	[ ]	Identify people's problems	[ ]	[ ]	_____
[ ]	[ ]	Influence others	[ ]	[ ]	_____
[ ]	[ ]	Interview others	[ ]	[ ]	_____
[ ]	[ ]	Keep groups on track and moving	[ ]	[ ]	_____
			[ ]	[ ]	_____
[ ]	[ ]	Lead others	[ ]	[ ]	_____
[ ]	[ ]	Listen attentively	[ ]	[ ]	_____
[ ]	[ ]	Listen with empathy	[ ]	[ ]	_____
[ ]	[ ]	Manage conflict	[ ]	[ ]	_____
[ ]	[ ]	Manage people	[ ]	[ ]	_____

Functional Data Skills

Remember, check only those skills that you are motivated to use in your worklife.

Acceptable	Needs Development	"I like to or would like to…"	Acceptable	Needs Development	
[ ]	[ ]	Administer policies and programs	[ ]	[ ]	Forecast trends
[ ]	[ ]	Allocate resources	[ ]	[ ]	Gather information and data
[ ]	[ ]	Analyze facts and ideas	[ ]	[ ]	Implement/Follow through
[ ]	[ ]	Analyze financial data	[ ]	[ ]	Improvise
[ ]	[ ]	Analyze needs	[ ]	[ ]	Initiate and promote change
[ ]	[ ]	Analyze plans	[ ]	[ ]	Innovate
[ ]	[ ]	Anticipate problems	[ ]	[ ]	Interview for information
[ ]	[ ]	Arrange events	[ ]	[ ]	Invent
[ ]	[ ]	Assess art	[ ]	[ ]	Inventory
[ ]	[ ]	Attend to details	[ ]	[ ]	Investigate
[ ]	[ ]	Brainstorm	[ ]	[ ]	Keep financial books
[ ]	[ ]	Calculate risks	[ ]	[ ]	Keep records
[ ]	[ ]	Champion a cause	[ ]	[ ]	Maintain schedules
[ ]	[ ]	Classify things and ideas	[ ]	[ ]	Make decisions
[ ]	[ ]	Compute	[ ]	[ ]	Manage budgets
[ ]	[ ]	Conceive, create, and develop ideas	[ ]	[ ]	Manage logistics
[ ]	[ ]	Conceptualize	[ ]	[ ]	Manage projects
[ ]	[ ]	Control inventory	[ ]	[ ]	Match people to tasks
[ ]	[ ]	Coordinate events and operations	[ ]	[ ]	Monitor and regulate work flow
[ ]	[ ]	Critique performance	[ ]	[ ]	Navigate a course
[ ]	[ ]	Critique writing	[ ]	[ ]	Observe details
[ ]	[ ]	Delegate responsibility	[ ]	[ ]	Operate computer terminal
[ ]	[ ]	Design architecture	[ ]	[ ]	Organize projects
[ ]	[ ]	Design interiors	[ ]	[ ]	Organize information logically
[ ]	[ ]	Design and develop systems	[ ]	[ ]	Organize people
[ ]	[ ]	Design training programs	[ ]	[ ]	Perceive and define cause and effect relationships
[ ]	[ ]	Determine policy	[ ]	[ ]	Plan projects
[ ]	[ ]	Develop structure	[ ]	[ ]	Plan strategically
[ ]	[ ]	Diagnose problems	[ ]	[ ]	Plan work assignments
[ ]	[ ]	Do pricing	[ ]	[ ]	Prepare budgets
[ ]	[ ]	Edit and proofread	[ ]	[ ]	Prepare financial data
[ ]	[ ]	Establish procedures	[ ]	[ ]	Present information logically
[ ]	[ ]	Estimate material quantities	[ ]	[ ]	Produce events
[ ]	[ ]	Estimate costs	[ ]	[ ]	Provide organizational structure
[ ]	[ ]	Evaluate data and ideas	[ ]	[ ]	Purchase materials
[ ]	[ ]	Expedite	[ ]	[ ]	Read technical information
[ ]	[ ]	Follow instructions			

Remember, check only those skills that you are motivated to use in your worklife.

Acceptable	Needs Development	"I like to or would like to…"	Acceptable	Needs Development	
[ ]	[ ]	Research subjects	[ ]	[ ]	_____
[ ]	[ ]	Solve math problems	[ ]	[ ]	_____
[ ]	[ ]	Solve problems	[ ]	[ ]	_____
[ ]	[ ]	Solve statistical problems	[ ]	[ ]	_____
[ ]	[ ]	Synthesize facts and ideas	[ ]	[ ]	_____
[ ]	[ ]	Systematize materials and operations	[ ]	[ ]	_____
[ ]	[ ]	Think logically	[ ]	[ ]	_____
[ ]	[ ]	Troubleshoot and correct problems	[ ]	[ ]	_____
[ ]	[ ]	Understand complex material	[ ]	[ ]	_____
[ ]	[ ]	Understand finances	[ ]	[ ]	_____
[ ]	[ ]	Use intuition	[ ]	[ ]	_____
[ ]	[ ]	Use mathematics	[ ]	[ ]	_____
[ ]	[ ]	Use statistics	[ ]	[ ]	_____
[ ]	[ ]	Work with abstract material/concepts	[ ]	[ ]	_____
[ ]	[ ]	Work with blueprints	[ ]	[ ]	_____
[ ]	[ ]	Work within structure	[ ]	[ ]	_____
[ ]	[ ]	Write creatively	[ ]	[ ]	_____
[ ]	[ ]	Write promotion and publicity	[ ]	[ ]	_____
[ ]	[ ]	Write proposals	[ ]	[ ]	_____
[ ]	[ ]	Write technical material	[ ]	[ ]	_____
[ ]	[ ]	_____	[ ]	[ ]	_____
[ ]	[ ]	_____	[ ]	[ ]	_____
[ ]	[ ]	_____	[ ]	[ ]	_____
[ ]	[ ]	_____	[ ]	[ ]	_____
[ ]	[ ]	_____	[ ]	[ ]	_____
[ ]	[ ]	_____	[ ]	[ ]	_____
[ ]	[ ]	_____	[ ]	[ ]	_____
[ ]	[ ]	_____	[ ]	[ ]	_____
[ ]	[ ]	_____	[ ]	[ ]	_____
[ ]	[ ]	_____	[ ]	[ ]	_____
[ ]	[ ]	_____	[ ]	[ ]	_____
[ ]	[ ]	_____	[ ]	[ ]	_____
[ ]	[ ]	_____	[ ]	[ ]	_____
[ ]	[ ]	_____	[ ]	[ ]	_____
[ ]	[ ]	_____	[ ]	[ ]	_____
[ ]	[ ]	_____	[ ]	[ ]	_____
[ ]	[ ]	_____	[ ]	[ ]	_____

[√] Functional Thing Skills

Remember, check only those skills that you are motivated to use in your worklife.

Acceptable	Needs Development	"I like to or would like to…"	Acceptable	Needs Development	
[ ]	[ ]	Assemble things	[ ]	[ ]	Survive in the wilderness
[ ]	[ ]	Be athletic	[ ]	[ ]	Take care of living things
[ ]	[ ]	Build with wood	[ ]	[ ]	Take quality photographs
[ ]	[ ]	Clean thoroughly	[ ]	[ ]	Type
[ ]	[ ]	Construct things	[ ]	[ ]	Use finger dexterity
[ ]	[ ]	Cook	[ ]	[ ]	Use hand tools
[ ]	[ ]	Dance	[ ]	[ ]	Use manual dexterity
[ ]	[ ]	Design furniture	[ ]	[ ]	Use physical strength
[ ]	[ ]	Diagnose mechanical problems	[ ]	[ ]	Use power tools
			[ ]	[ ]	Use weapons
[ ]	[ ]	Display things	[ ]	[ ]	Visualize size and shape
[ ]	[ ]	Do body work	[ ]	[ ]	Work outdoors
[ ]	[ ]	Do carpentry	[ ]	[ ]	Work with animals
[ ]	[ ]	Do craft work	[ ]	[ ]	Work with instruments
[ ]	[ ]	Do electrical work	[ ]	[ ]	Work with machines
[ ]	[ ]	Do farming	[ ]	[ ]	Work with nature
[ ]	[ ]	Do ironwork	[ ]	[ ]	_____
[ ]	[ ]	Do masonry	[ ]	[ ]	_____
[ ]	[ ]	Do plumbing	[ ]	[ ]	_____
[ ]	[ ]	Do precision work	[ ]	[ ]	_____
[ ]	[ ]	Do sheet-metal work	[ ]	[ ]	_____
[ ]	[ ]	Drafting	[ ]	[ ]	_____
[ ]	[ ]	Draw illustrations	[ ]	[ ]	_____
[ ]	[ ]	Drive heavy equipment	[ ]	[ ]	_____
[ ]	[ ]	Drive vehicles	[ ]	[ ]	_____
[ ]	[ ]	Garden	[ ]	[ ]	_____
[ ]	[ ]	Grow things	[ ]	[ ]	_____
[ ]	[ ]	Have good spatial perception	[ ]	[ ]	_____
[ ]	[ ]	Inspect construction	[ ]	[ ]	_____
[ ]	[ ]	Lay bricks	[ ]	[ ]	_____
[ ]	[ ]	Maintain equipment	[ ]	[ ]	_____
[ ]	[ ]	Maintain physical stamina	[ ]	[ ]	_____
[ ]	[ ]	Move with good physical coordination	[ ]	[ ]	_____
[ ]	[ ]	Operate office equipment	[ ]	[ ]	_____
[ ]	[ ]	Paint	[ ]	[ ]	_____
[ ]	[ ]	Play a musical instrument	[ ]	[ ]	_____
[ ]	[ ]	Repair things	[ ]	[ ]	_____
[ ]	[ ]	Sculpt	[ ]	[ ]	_____
[ ]	[ ]	Sort	[ ]	[ ]	_____

Most Important Functional Skills Currently at an Acceptable Level of Development

From the lists that you just checked, select up to five people skills, five data skills, and five thing skills that you would most like to include in your worklife, and which are currently at an acceptable level of development. You need not include all three categories if you wish to concentrate on only one or two. Write them in order of enjoyment. You can include more than one skill on a line if you feel they are related and form a skill cluster.

People Skills

1. _____

2. _____

3. _____

4. _____

5. _____

Data Skills

1. _____

2. _____

3. _____

4. _____

5. _____

Thing Skills

1. _____

2. _____

3. _____

4. _____

5. _____

Most Important Functional Skills Currently in Need of Development

From the lists that you just checked, select up to five people skills, five data skills, and five thing skills that you would most like to include in your worklife, and which you checked as needing development. You need not include all three categories if you wish to concentrate on only one or two. Write them in order of your perceived need for development. You can include more than one skill on a line if you feel they are related and form a skill cluster.

People Skills

1. _____

2. _____

3. _____

4. _____

5. _____

Data Skills

1. _____

2. _____

3. _____

4. _____

5. _____

Thing Skills

1. _____

2. _____

3. _____

4. _____

5. _____

Assessing Your Adaptive Skills (Positive Personal Qualities and Characteristics)

*R*ecognition of your positive personal qualities and characteristics is critically important in building self esteem. The expression of these characteristics plays a key role in work effectiveness, performance, and job satisfaction.

Therefore, we have included an extensive list of these personal qualities. The list has been developed with some redundancy or overlap. There are different ways of saying and perceiving things that may be more familiar to you and make it easier for you to relate to and recognize an item as one of your adaptive skills. It's all right for there to be some duplication in your checked list of characteristics.

It is informative and interesting to compare your adaptive skills with the information you discovered about yourself in the previous chapters on Style and Career Type. As you continue to complete the overall picture, you will notice certain pieces falling into place. These suggested comparisons will help you to focus on what is really true for you and will serve to support you in writing a more comprehensive and accurate *Personal Career Profile*.

Read through the following lists and for those qualities that you prefer to have in your worklife check whether the level at which you currently exercise that quality is acceptable or needs development. Do not be overly judgmental or perfectionistic, or think in all-or-nothing terms. Space is also provided for you to add qualities that may not be included on these lists. When you read through the qualities, think - "I am (or have) or would like to be (or to have)…" and complete the sentence with the appropriate qualities from the lists.

80

[√] *Adaptive Skills/Personal Qualities*

Remember, check only those qualities that you are motivated to use in your worklife.

Acceptable	Needs Development	"I am (or have) or would like to be (or to have)…"	Acceptable	Needs Development	
[ ]	[ ]	Able to admit mistakes	[ ]	[ ]	Broad-minded
[ ]	[ ]	Able to "deliver" on time	[ ]	[ ]	Business-like
[ ]	[ ]	Able to get to the heart of problems	[ ]	[ ]	Bold
			[ ]	[ ]	Calm
[ ]	[ ]	Able to "follow-through"	[ ]	[ ]	Candid in dealing with others
[ ]	[ ]	Able to express feelings in an open and direct manner	[ ]	[ ]	Capable
			[ ]	[ ]	Careful
[ ]	[ ]	Able to express ideas freely	[ ]	[ ]	Caring
[ ]	[ ]	Able to get along well with others	[ ]	[ ]	Cautious
			[ ]	[ ]	Challenge-seeking
[ ]	[ ]	Able to maintain temper in face of provocation	[ ]	[ ]	Charismatic
			[ ]	[ ]	Cheerful
[ ]	[ ]	Able to plan effectively	[ ]	[ ]	Clear thinking
[ ]	[ ]	Able to set priorities well	[ ]	[ ]	Clever
[ ]	[ ]	Able to take criticism	[ ]	[ ]	Committed to personal growth
[ ]	[ ]	Able to think things out before acting	[ ]	[ ]	Communicative
			[ ]	[ ]	Compassionate
[ ]	[ ]	Able to think quickly on my feet	[ ]	[ ]	Competent
			[ ]	[ ]	Competitive
[ ]	[ ]	Able to use time effectively	[ ]	[ ]	Concentration
[ ]	[ ]	Able to work well in structured environment	[ ]	[ ]	Concern for others
			[ ]	[ ]	Concise
[ ]	[ ]	Able to work well under stress	[ ]	[ ]	Confident
[ ]	[ ]	Academic	[ ]	[ ]	Congenial
[ ]	[ ]	Accepting	[ ]	[ ]	Conscientious
[ ]	[ ]	Accurate	[ ]	[ ]	Conservative in thought
[ ]	[ ]	Achievement oriented	[ ]	[ ]	Considerate
[ ]	[ ]	Action oriented	[ ]	[ ]	Consistent
[ ]	[ ]	Active	[ ]	[ ]	Cool under fire
[ ]	[ ]	Adaptable to change	[ ]	[ ]	Cooperative
[ ]	[ ]	Adventurous	[ ]	[ ]	Cost conscious
[ ]	[ ]	Aggressive	[ ]	[ ]	Courageous
[ ]	[ ]	Alert	[ ]	[ ]	Creative
[ ]	[ ]	Ambitious	[ ]	[ ]	Credible
[ ]	[ ]	Analytical	[ ]	[ ]	Curious
[ ]	[ ]	Assertive	[ ]	[ ]	Daring
[ ]	[ ]	Astute	[ ]	[ ]	Decisive
[ ]	[ ]	Attentive to details	[ ]	[ ]	Dedicated to organizations
[ ]	[ ]	Authentic	[ ]	[ ]	Dedicated to personal goals
[ ]	[ ]	Balanced life	[ ]	[ ]	Deliberate

81

Remember, check only those qualities that you are motivated to use in your worklife.

Acceptable	Needs Development	*"I am (or have) or would like to be (or to have)..."*	Acceptable	Needs Development	
[ ]	[ ]	Demanding of self	[ ]	[ ]	Genuine
[ ]	[ ]	Dependable	[ ]	[ ]	Goal-oriented
[ ]	[ ]	Detail-oriented	[ ]	[ ]	Good ego strength
[ ]	[ ]	Determined	[ ]	[ ]	Good follow-through
[ ]	[ ]	Dexterous	[ ]	[ ]	Good judge of others
[ ]	[ ]	Diligent	[ ]	[ ]	Good judgment
[ ]	[ ]	Diplomatic	[ ]	[ ]	Good listener
[ ]	[ ]	Direct	[ ]	[ ]	Good sense of self
[ ]	[ ]	Discreet	[ ]	[ ]	Good team player
[ ]	[ ]	Dynamic	[ ]	[ ]	Gregarious
[ ]	[ ]	Eager	[ ]	[ ]	Hardworking
[ ]	[ ]	Easily stimulated	[ ]	[ ]	Healthy
[ ]	[ ]	Easygoing	[ ]	[ ]	Helpful
[ ]	[ ]	Economical	[ ]	[ ]	High energy
[ ]	[ ]	Effective problem solver	[ ]	[ ]	Honest
[ ]	[ ]	Efficient	[ ]	[ ]	Humanistic
[ ]	[ ]	Emotionally stable	[ ]	[ ]	Idealistic
[ ]	[ ]	Empathetic	[ ]	[ ]	Imaginative
[ ]	[ ]	Encouraging of others	[ ]	[ ]	Independent
[ ]	[ ]	Endurance	[ ]	[ ]	Individualistic
[ ]	[ ]	Energetic	[ ]	[ ]	Industrious
[ ]	[ ]	Enterprising	[ ]	[ ]	Informal
[ ]	[ ]	Enthusiastic	[ ]	[ ]	Initiative
[ ]	[ ]	Entrepreneurial	[ ]	[ ]	Innovative
[ ]	[ ]	Exacting	[ ]	[ ]	Insightful
[ ]	[ ]	Excited about challenge	[ ]	[ ]	Insight into my own motives and behaviors
[ ]	[ ]	Expressive			
[ ]	[ ]	Factual	[ ]	[ ]	Integrity
[ ]	[ ]	Fair-minded	[ ]	[ ]	Intellectual
[ ]	[ ]	Faithful	[ ]	[ ]	Intelligent
[ ]	[ ]	Far-sighted	[ ]	[ ]	In touch with my feelings
[ ]	[ ]	Fast thinking on my feet	[ ]	[ ]	Introspective
[ ]	[ ]	Firm	[ ]	[ ]	Intuitive
[ ]	[ ]	Flexible	[ ]	[ ]	Inventive
[ ]	[ ]	Forceful	[ ]	[ ]	Involved
[ ]	[ ]	Foresighted	[ ]	[ ]	Kind
[ ]	[ ]	Frank	[ ]	[ ]	Knowledgeable about myself
[ ]	[ ]	Friendly	[ ]	[ ]	Knowledgeable about the world
[ ]	[ ]	Frugal			
[ ]	[ ]	Generous	[ ]	[ ]	Level-headed

82

**Remember, check only those qualities that you
are motivated to use in your worklife.**

Acceptable	Needs Development	"I am (or have) or would like to be (or to have)…"	Acceptable	Needs Development	
[ ]	[ ]	Likable	[ ]	[ ]	Practical
[ ]	[ ]	Logical	[ ]	[ ]	Precise
[ ]	[ ]	Loving	[ ]	[ ]	Proactive
[ ]	[ ]	Loyal	[ ]	[ ]	Problem solver
[ ]	[ ]	Mature	[ ]	[ ]	Productive
[ ]	[ ]	Methodical	[ ]	[ ]	Professional
[ ]	[ ]	Meticulous	[ ]	[ ]	Progressive
[ ]	[ ]	Modest	[ ]	[ ]	Project oriented
[ ]	[ ]	Moral	[ ]	[ ]	Prudent
[ ]	[ ]	Motivated	[ ]	[ ]	Punctual
[ ]	[ ]	Motivating	[ ]	[ ]	Purposeful
[ ]	[ ]	Natural	[ ]	[ ]	Quick learner
[ ]	[ ]	Neat and clean	[ ]	[ ]	Quick to take initiative
[ ]	[ ]	Nurturing	[ ]	[ ]	Rational
[ ]	[ ]	Objective	[ ]	[ ]	Realistic
[ ]	[ ]	Observant	[ ]	[ ]	Reasonable
[ ]	[ ]	Open to ideas	[ ]	[ ]	Reflective
[ ]	[ ]	Open to others	[ ]	[ ]	Relaxed
[ ]	[ ]	Open-minded	[ ]	[ ]	Reliable
[ ]	[ ]	Optimistic	[ ]	[ ]	Reserved
[ ]	[ ]	Orderly	[ ]	[ ]	Resilient
[ ]	[ ]	Organized	[ ]	[ ]	Resourceful
[ ]	[ ]	Original	[ ]	[ ]	Responsible
[ ]	[ ]	Outgoing	[ ]	[ ]	Responsive
[ ]	[ ]	Outspoken	[ ]	[ ]	Results-oriented
[ ]	[ ]	Patient	[ ]	[ ]	Risk-taker
[ ]	[ ]	People-oriented	[ ]	[ ]	Secure
[ ]	[ ]	Perceptive	[ ]	[ ]	Self-accepting
[ ]	[ ]	Perform well under stress	[ ]	[ ]	Self-analytical
[ ]	[ ]	Persevering	[ ]	[ ]	Self-assured
[ ]	[ ]	Persistent	[ ]	[ ]	Self-aware
[ ]	[ ]	Personable	[ ]	[ ]	Self-confident
[ ]	[ ]	Persuasive	[ ]	[ ]	Self-controlled
[ ]	[ ]	Physically attractive	[ ]	[ ]	Self-correcting
[ ]	[ ]	Physically strong	[ ]	[ ]	Self-directed
[ ]	[ ]	Playful	[ ]	[ ]	Self-disciplined
[ ]	[ ]	Poised	[ ]	[ ]	Self-expressive
[ ]	[ ]	Polished	[ ]	[ ]	Self-improvement oriented
[ ]	[ ]	Politically aware	[ ]	[ ]	Self-motivated
[ ]	[ ]	Positive	[ ]	[ ]	Self-reliant

83

Remember, check only those qualities that you are motivated to use in your worklife.

Acceptable	Needs Development	"I am (or have) or would like to be (or to have)…"	Acceptable	Needs Development	
[ ]	[ ]	Self-starting	[ ]	[ ]	Unexcitable
[ ]	[ ]	Self-sufficient	[ ]	[ ]	Understanding
[ ]	[ ]	Sense-of-humor	[ ]	[ ]	Uninhibited
[ ]	[ ]	Sensible	[ ]	[ ]	Unpretentious
[ ]	[ ]	Sensitive to others	[ ]	[ ]	Unselfish
[ ]	[ ]	Sensitive to political climate	[ ]	[ ]	Venturesome
[ ]	[ ]	Serious-minded	[ ]	[ ]	Verbal
[ ]	[ ]	Service oriented	[ ]	[ ]	Versatile
[ ]	[ ]	Shrewd	[ ]	[ ]	Warm
[ ]	[ ]	Sincere	[ ]	[ ]	Well groomed
[ ]	[ ]	Sociable	[ ]	[ ]	Wholesome
[ ]	[ ]	Socially adept	[ ]	[ ]	Willing to learn
[ ]	[ ]	Sophisticated	[ ]	[ ]	Willing to seek and take responsibility
[ ]	[ ]	Sound judgment			
[ ]	[ ]	Spontaneous	[ ]	[ ]	Willing to work steadily for distant goals
[ ]	[ ]	Stable			
[ ]	[ ]	Steady	[ ]	[ ]	Wise
[ ]	[ ]	Straight-forward	[ ]	[ ]	Witty
[ ]	[ ]	Strong sense of conviction	[ ]	[ ]	_____
[ ]	[ ]	Strong-willed (determined)	[ ]	[ ]	_____
[ ]	[ ]	Supportive of others	[ ]	[ ]	_____
[ ]	[ ]	Sympathetic	[ ]	[ ]	_____
[ ]	[ ]	Systematic	[ ]	[ ]	_____
[ ]	[ ]	Tactful	[ ]	[ ]	_____
[ ]	[ ]	Task oriented	[ ]	[ ]	_____
[ ]	[ ]	Team player	[ ]	[ ]	_____
[ ]	[ ]	Tenacious	[ ]	[ ]	_____
[ ]	[ ]	Thorough	[ ]	[ ]	_____
[ ]	[ ]	Thoughtful	[ ]	[ ]	_____
[ ]	[ ]	Thoughtful of others	[ ]	[ ]	_____
[ ]	[ ]	Thrifty	[ ]	[ ]	_____
[ ]	[ ]	Tidy	[ ]	[ ]	_____
[ ]	[ ]	Tolerant of ambiguity	[ ]	[ ]	_____
[ ]	[ ]	Tolerant of others mistakes	[ ]	[ ]	_____
[ ]	[ ]	Tolerant of routine	[ ]	[ ]	_____
[ ]	[ ]	Tough-minded	[ ]	[ ]	_____
[ ]	[ ]	Trusting	[ ]	[ ]	_____
[ ]	[ ]	Trustworthy	[ ]	[ ]	_____
[ ]	[ ]	Unaffected	[ ]	[ ]	_____
[ ]	[ ]	Unassuming	[ ]	[ ]	_____

*F*rom the lists that you just checked, select up to 15 adaptive skills/ personal qualities that you would most like to use in your worklife, and which you consider to be currently at an acceptable level of development. If several adaptive skills appear the same or similar, group them together on a single line to form one cluster or family of related qualities. Use up to 15 lines.

Priority   **Adaptive Skills**

[ ] _____

[ ] _____

[ ] _____

[ ] _____

[ ] _____

[ ] _____

[ ] _____

[ ] _____

[ ] _____

[ ] _____

[ ] _____

[ ] _____

[ ] _____

[ ] _____

[ ] _____

Write a 1 in the space to the left of the quality you consider to be your strongest, a 2 for the next most important quality, etc., until you have selected your five most important adaptive skills/personal qualities.

[√] *Most Important Adaptive Skills Currently in Need of Development*

From the lists that you just checked, select up to 15 adaptive skills/ personal qualities that you would most like to use in your worklife, and which you consider to need development. If several adaptive skills appear the same or similar, group them together on a single line to form one cluster or family of related qualities. Use up to 15 lines.

Priority   ***Adaptive Skills***

[   ] _____

[   ] _____

[   ] _____

[   ] _____

[   ] _____

[   ] _____

[   ] _____

[   ] _____

[   ] _____

[   ] _____

[   ] _____

[   ] _____

[   ] _____

[   ] _____

[   ] _____

Write a 1 in the space to the left of the quality you consider to be most in need of development, a 2 for the next most important quality, etc., until you have selected your five most important adaptive skills/ personal qualities currently in need of development.

[√] *Internal Barriers*   6

*T*o be complete, any exploration of who you are must include an inventory of internal barriers – those blocks or stops that you use to keep yourself from being who you want to be, doing what you want to do, and having what you want to have.

Internal Barriers and Problematic Personality Characteristics

*T*hese barriers take the form of attitudes, behavior patterns, rigid beliefs, fears, or real or imagined deficiencies in your skills. While it may not be possible to eliminate all of these barriers, it is possible to manage them, or at least move ahead in spite of them. By telling the truth about the existence of a specific barrier you can begin the process of reducing its effects. The conscious awareness of a barrier allows you to observe how and when it serves as a block and gives you the opportunity to modify attitudes and behaviors in favor of being more effective in being, doing, and having what you want.

The first step is to tell the truth about your barriers. This may be a difficult or upsetting process! It is important, however, to accept yourself exactly as you are right now. This self-acceptance is the starting point for all self-improvement. Recognize that everyone has barriers, and that only those who are willing to acknowledge them can successfully manage the barriers in a way that expands their lives. References to information on self-improvement and dealing with barriers are included in the selected reading materials at the end of this book.

If in the course of getting in touch with your internal barriers you become troubled or depressed, we would encourage you to seek professional counseling in dealing with these feelings. Counseling can enable you to maximize your potential for happiness, fulfillment, and professional satisfaction.

Assessing Your Internal Barriers

Read through the list of internal barriers and problematic personality characteristics on the following pages and check those that you feel currently give you difficulty on your job or in your life. Space is provided for you to add any barriers that have not been included on the list.

The list of internal barriers has been developed with some redundancy or overlap. There are different ways of saying and perceiving things that may be more familiar to you and make it easier for you to recognize an item as one of your internal barriers. It's all right for there to be some duplication in your checked list of barriers. Most people check over 25 internal barriers applicable to themselves.

Internal barriers are often reflective of your style characteristics rather than personal deficiencies. It is informative and interesting to compare your internal barriers with the information you discovered about yourself in the previous chapters on Style and Career Type. As you continue to complete the overall picture, you will notice certain pieces falling into place. These suggested comparisons will help you to focus on what is really true for you and will serve to support you in writing a more comprehensive and accurate *Personal Career Profile*.

[√] *Internal Barriers*

Remember, check only those barriers that currently give you difficulty in your worklife.

"I am, or I have..."

[ ] Abrasive
[ ] Abrupt
[ ] Absent-minded
[ ] "All-or-nothing" behavior
[ ] Aloof
[ ] Argumentative
[ ] Ambivalent
[ ] An unclear sense of identity
[ ] Anger (uncontrolled)
[ ] Antisocial
[ ] Anxious
[ ] Apathetic
[ ] Arrogant
[ ] Autocratic
[ ] Bitter
[ ] "Black-or-white" thinking
[ ] Blaming of others
[ ] Boastful
[ ] Boring
[ ] Bossy and dominating
[ ] Burnt out
[ ] Careless
[ ] Closed-minded
[ ] Coarse
[ ] Cold-hearted
[ ] Complaining
[ ] Compulsive
[ ] Conceited
[ ] Conflicting values
[ ] Confronting to others
[ ] Confused self-image
[ ] Constricted
[ ] Cynical
[ ] Deceitful
[ ] Defensive
[ ] Delusional
[ ] Depressed often
[ ] Dictatorial
[ ] Difficulty being competitive
[ ] Difficulty developing reasonable personal expectations

[ ] Difficulty expressing anger
[ ] Difficulty expressing feelings in general
[ ] Difficulty getting organized
[ ] Difficulty in generating alternatives
[ ] Difficulty in managing details
[ ] Difficulty listening well
[ ] Difficulty making decisions
[ ] Difficulty managing stress and pressure
[ ] Difficulty managing time
[ ] Difficulty planning ahead
[ ] Difficulty relating well to others
[ ] Difficulty selling myself
[ ] Difficulty setting priorities
[ ] Difficulty sustaining concentration
[ ] Difficulty with ambiguity or uncertainty
[ ] Difficulty with authority
[ ] Difficulty with lack of structure
[ ] Difficulty with rejection
[ ] Difficulty with structure
[ ] Difficulty with taking criticism
[ ] Diffuse and scattered
[ ] Disorganized
[ ] Distrustful of others
[ ] Dogmatic
[ ] Dull and overly methodical
[ ] Easily bored
[ ] Easily discouraged
[ ] Easily distracted
[ ] Easily frustrated
[ ] Easily hurt feelings
[ ] Easily irritated
[ ] Easily overwhelmed
[ ] Egocentric
[ ] Egotistical
[ ] Envious
[ ] Erratic
[ ] Excessive concern with what others think of me

Remember, check only those barriers that currently give you difficulty in your worklife.

"I am, or I have..."

[ ] Excessive daydreams and fantasies
[ ] Excessive distrust of intuition
[ ] Excessive distrust of others
[ ] Excessive distrust of technology
[ ] Excessive guilt feelings
[ ] Excessive need for attention
[ ] Excessive need for certainty
[ ] Excessive need for control
[ ] Excessive need for external validation
[ ] Excessive need for security
[ ] Excessive need of approval
[ ] Excessive need to please others
[ ] Excessively competitive
[ ] Excessively demanding of myself
[ ] Excessively fault-finding
[ ] Excessively self-critical
[ ] Excessively self-involved
[ ] Fear masquerading as laziness
[ ] Fear of age limitations
[ ] Fear of appearing weak
[ ] Fear of authority
[ ] Fear of being at financial risk
[ ] Fear of being myself
[ ] Fear of change
[ ] Fear of closing options
[ ] Fear of commitment
[ ] Fear of competition
[ ] Fear of failure
[ ] Fear of financial insecurity
[ ] Fear of hurting others
[ ] Fear of looking foolish
[ ] Fear of losing
[ ] Fear of making mistakes
[ ] Fear of promotion
[ ] Fear of public speaking
[ ] Fear of risk-taking
[ ] Fear of success
[ ] Fear of taking responsibility
[ ] Fear of technology
[ ] Fear of the unknown

[ ] Feelings of being an imposter or fraud
[ ] Feelings of being unsophisticated
[ ] Feelings of inadequacy
[ ] Frequent feelings of being a victim
[ ] Financial insecurity
[ ] Flighty
[ ] Forgetful
[ ] Fussy
[ ] Generally fearful
[ ] Generous to a fault
[ ] Greedy
[ ] Hard-headed
[ ] Haughty
[ ] High-strung
[ ] Hostile toward others
[ ] Hypersensitive
[ ] Immature
[ ] Impatient
[ ] Impulsive
[ ] Inability to self-evaluate performance
[ ] Inconsistent
[ ] Indecisive
[ ] Indiscreet
[ ] Inflexible
[ ] Inhibiting self-doubt
[ ] Insensitive to needs and feelings of others
[ ] Intolerant
[ ] Irresponsible
[ ] Irritable
[ ] Irritatingly "offbeat"
[ ] Jealous
[ ] Lack of assertiveness
[ ] Lack of confidence
[ ] Lack of diplomacy
[ ] Lack of follow-through
[ ] Lack of goals
[ ] Lack of motivation
[ ] Lack of persistence

90

Remember, check only those barriers that currently give you difficulty in your worklife.

"I am, or I have..."

[   ] Lack of social skills
[   ] Lack of spontaneity
[   ] Lack of tact
[   ] Lack of vision
[   ] Lazy
[   ] Limited attention span
[   ] Low frustration tolerance
[   ] Low self-esteem
[   ] Low stress tolerance
[   ] Manipulative
[   ] Meek
[   ] Moody
[   ] Naive politically
[   ] Naive socially
[   ] Narcissistic
[   ] Need for guarantees
[   ] Need for excessive positive
       reinforcement from others
[   ] Need for immediate gratification
[   ] Need to compare self to others
[   ] Negative self-concept
[   ] Negativistic
[   ] Nervous
[   ] Nosy
[   ] Obnoxious
[   ] Opinionated (overly)
[   ] Out of touch with my feelings
[   ] Overly aggressive
[   ] Overly anxious to please
[   ] Overly blunt
[   ] Overly cautious
[   ] Overly concerned with details
[   ] Overly compliant
[   ] Overly controlled
[   ] Overly controlling of others
[   ] Overly critical
[   ] Overly dependent
[   ] Overly detached
[   ] Overly eager to impress others
[   ] Overly emotional
[   ] Overly inhibited

[   ] Overly judgmental
[   ] Overly passive
[   ] Overly pessimistic
[   ] Overly reactive
[   ] Overly ready to take on guilt
[   ] Overly restricting belief systems
[   ] Overly skeptical
[   ] Overly suggestible
[   ] Overly talkative
[   ] Overly task oriented
[   ] Overly temperamental
[   ] Overly trusting
[   ] Paranoid
[   ] Perfectionism
[   ] Physical fear
[   ] Plateaued
[   ] Poor ego strength
[   ] Poor judge of other people
[   ] Poor listening skills
[   ] Poor physical health
[   ] Poor self-control
[   ] Poor self-discipline
[   ] Poor self-management
[   ] Poor sense of appropriate
       appearance
[   ] Prejudiced
[   ] Preoccupied with self
[   ] Problems being competitive
[   ] Procrastination
[   ] Prone to vacillation
[   ] Quick to anger
[   ] Reactive instead of proactive
[   ] Rebellious
[   ] Resistance to new ideas and
       people
[   ] Restless
[   ] Rigid
[   ] Sarcastic
[   ] Self-denying
[   ] Self-doubt
[   ] Self-indulgent

91

Remember, check only those barriers that currently give you difficulty in your worklife.

"I am, or I have…"

[ ] Selfish
[ ] Self-pitying
[ ] Self-sabotaging
[ ] Sense of lack of creativity
[ ] Shallow
[ ] Short tempered
[ ] "Should-or-ought" thinking
[ ] Show-off
[ ] Shy to an extreme
[ ] Skeptical
[ ] Slow to forgive
[ ] Slow to see humor
[ ] Smug
[ ] Snobbish
[ ] Socially awkward
[ ] Stubborn
[ ] Stingy
[ ] Strong need to prove myself
[ ] Submissive
[ ] Substance abuse
[ ] Sulky
[ ] Suspicious of others' motives
[ ] Tendency to delay or avoid action
[ ] Tendency to hold everything in
[ ] Tendency to keep people at a distance and avoid close relationships
[ ] Tendency to personalize things
[ ] Tendency to take path of least resistance
[ ] Tendency to obsess about things
[ ] Tendency to vacillate
[ ] Tense
[ ] Thin-skinned
[ ] Tight control over feelings and emotions
[ ] Timid
[ ] Too ready to avoid conflict
[ ] Touchy
[ ] Unaware of my impact on others
[ ] Undependable

[ ] Underachiever
[ ] Uneasy about physical appearance
[ ] Uninterested in others
[ ] Uninvolved
[ ] Unmotivated
[ ] Unrealistic
[ ] Unrealistic expectation of others
[ ] Unrealistic expectation of myself
[ ] Unreasonable
[ ] Unresponsive
[ ] Untidy
[ ] Values conflicts
[ ] Vindictive
[ ] Vulnerable to real or imagined threats
[ ] Withdrawn
[ ] Workaholic
[ ] Worrisome
[ ] _____
[ ] _____
[ ] _____
[ ] _____
[ ] _____
[ ] _____
[ ] _____
[ ] _____
[ ] _____
[ ] _____
[ ] _____
[ ] _____
[ ] _____
[ ] _____
[ ] _____
[ ] _____
[ ] _____
[ ] _____
[ ] _____

[√] *Most Important Internal Barriers Currently in Need of Reduction or Elimination*

From the list that you just checked, select up to 15 work-related internal barriers that you would most like to reduce or eliminate from your work or life. If several words are similar in meaning, group them together and include them on a single line to form a cluster or family of internal barriers. Use up to 15 lines

Priority

[ ] _____

[ ] _____

[ ] _____

[ ] _____

[ ] _____

[ ] _____

[ ] _____

[ ] _____

[ ] _____

[ ] _____

[ ] _____

[ ] _____

[ ] _____

[ ] _____

[ ] _____

93

Write a 1 in the space to the left of the barrier you consider to be your greatest work-related internal barrier, a 2 for the next most important barrier, etc., until you have identified your five most important work-related internal barriers currently in need of reduction or elimination.

[√] *Personal Career Profile*

After the significant amount of work that you have invested in discovering who you are in relation to your worklife, it will be extremely valuable to put it all together in a concise, readable, and usable way.

Putting It All Together

The *Personal Career Profile* has been developed to allow you to summarize all of the information developed so that you can go to a single document that clearly expresses who you are. The *Personal Career Profile* is not a resume. It does not contain your work history or education. It says more about you in the deeper context of your life and work. It is more like a multi-dimensional x-ray or "Career CAT-Scan" that provides you and anyone else you want to show it to with a deep image of who you are, a statement of your core self-identity in relation to your career and worklife.

Take your time putting the profile together. Follow the directions carefully, read the examples, work on drafts, and make sure you are satisfied with the version you consider final. Take liberties with the format if doing so provides you with a clearer and more useful description of your profile. Of course you can always go back and rewrite your profile, but if you do it well the first time, you will find it useful for a long time and for many purposes.

Good luck and enjoy this completion of all of your hard work.

Your Concise Personal Career Profile

The diagram on page 97 will be used to create a concise version of your *Personal Career Profile*. A more detailed version will follow. The following directions will assist you in completing the concise form.

1. *Style.* Write the four-letter code for your *Type* from page 16 in the chapter on Style in the four boxes provided. In the lines provided, write in five key words or phrases from the description of your style (also from page 16 in the chapter on Style) that you consider to best describe your style.

2. *Career Types.* Write the three-letter code for your *Career Types* from page 38 in the chapter on Career Type in the three boxes provided. In the lines provided, write in five key words or phrases from the description of your types (also from page 38 in the chapter on Career Type) that you consider to best describe your types.

3. *Career Anchor.* Write the name of your primary and secondary *Career Anchors* from page 54 in the chapter on Motivation in the space provided. In the lines provided, write in five key words or phrases from the description of your anchor (also from page 54 in the chapter on Motivation) that you consider to best describe your anchors.

4. **Most Important Values and Needs**. From page 68 in the chapter on Motivation, write in your five most important values and needs currently satisfied.

5. **Career Interests.** From page 39 in the chapter on Career Type, write in your five most appealing occupations, job titles, or broad areas of work.

6. **Most Important Motivated Functional Skills.** From page 78 in the chapter on Skills, write in your five most important people, data, and thing skills currently at an acceptable level of development.

7. **Most Important Motivated Adaptive Skills.** From page 85 in the chapter on Skills, write in your five most important adaptive skills/personal qualities currently at an acceptable level of development.

8. **Values and Needs Not Yet Satisfied.** From page 69 in the chapter on Motivation, write in your five most important values and needs not yet satisfied.

9. **Internal Barriers in Need of Reduction or Elimination.** From page 93 in the chapter on Internal Barriers, write in your five most important internal barriers currently in need of reduction or elimination.

10. **Functional Skill Developmental Needs.** From page 79 in the chapter on Skills, write in your five most important people, data, and thing skills currently in need of development.

11. **Adaptive Skill Developmental Needs.** From page 86 in the chapter on Skills, write in your five most important adaptive skills/personal qualities currently in need of development.

When you have completed this diagram, turn to the page following to begin a more detailed *Personal Career Profile*.

Concise Personal Career Profile

Style

1. Work Type

2. Career Type

Motivation

3. Career Anchor

PRIMARY

SECONDARY

4. Most Important Values & Needs

5. Career Interests

Skills

6. Most Important Motivated Functional Skills

PEOPLE   DATA   THINGS

7. Most Important Adaptive Skills

Developmental Needs

8. Values & Needs Not Yet Satisfied

9. Internal Barriers in Need of Reduction or Elimination

10. Functional Skill Developmental Needs

PEOPLE   DATA   THINGS

11. Adaptive Skill Developmental Needs

Your Detailed Personal Career Profile

*T*he *Concise Personal Career Profile* is intended to serve as a one-page description of you in relation to your worklife. It provides you with a simple and easily read overview that can be quickly referred to and understood.

In addition to this concise form, it is recommended that you prepare a more detailed profile. This detailed statement will help you to further build your self-awareness, self-esteem, and self-acceptance, as well as support you in making decisions. The detailed form will be useful to you in a variety of situations:

1. In the preparation of performance or development meetings with your manager.

2. As input to your career development planning – independently or in a formal course, program, or workshop.

3. In planning a development program.

4. In planning a career or job change.

5. In the preparation of resumes.

6. In the preparation of job interviews.

The principal format for the detailed profile is a narrative description of you in relation to your worklife, using the information you discovered in the assessments along with the descriptions provided of the various styles, types, anchors, etc. and any other ideas, thoughts, or feelings that arise as you write the profile. Career interests have been omitted from the detailed profile examples, but you may include them if you wish.

Detailed examples follow. Instructions are then provided to guide you through the writing of each section of the profile. It's a good idea to read one or more examples first before you move on to writing your own detailed profile. The instructions will then be more obvious and easier to follow. Please be aware that the examples provided are not intended to describe every person who holds the job title for which the profile has been written. It is perfectly appropriate if you are a mid-level corporate manager, for example, for your detailed profile to differ significantly from the one provided here. Again, take liberties with the format if doing so provides you with a clearer and more useful description of your profile.

[√] *Detailed Personal Career Profile Examples*

**Entrepreneur/
Small Business
Owner**

Style. My work type is ENTJ and my style is that of the "intuitive innovative organizer." I enjoy being an executive and running my own business. I like to think ahead, organize plans, and make a systematic effort to reach my objectives on schedule. I have always sought leadership roles, am frank in my expression, and have tried to be innovative in creating a vision for the future of organizations to which I belong. I like to be well-informed and enjoy adding to my fund of knowledge.

Career Type. My primary career type is "investigative." I am comfortable with abstractions, enjoy solving problems through the use of my analytical skills, love learning new things, and like to understand clearly how things work. I have been successful in an engineering job and have also worked as an engineering professor. In my current job, I am drawn to using computers and creating systems. My secondary career type is "enterprising." I am adventurous and drawn to power and leadership roles. I consider myself aggressive and self-confident, and have demonstrated social, leadership and speaking abilities. I have worked my way to the top of nearly every organization in which I have worked. My tertiary career type is "social." I am interested in other people and consider myself sensitive to their needs. I have taught professionally and value interpersonal relations. I often use my verbal and social skills to sell products and services to other people. I am cheerful, sometimes impulsive, and verbally oriented.

Career Anchor. My career anchor is "autonomy/independence." I am interested in doing things in my own way, on my own time, and as independently of others as possible. I would find belonging to or working for a large organization constraining. If I had to work for a big company I would be much happier as an independent contributor working on projects that I could create myself and for which I would have sole responsibility for the results. I also enjoy working in a situation where I can set my own projects, goals, hours, and ways of working. I own my own business because it gives me more freedom to do what I want. My autonomy is the last thing I would give up in making a job or career choice.

Values and Needs. My most important values include independence, full self-expression, creative expression, challenging problems, and high earnings. I am attempting to include these values in my work by owning my own business and spending as much time as possible in the area of developing new products through the exercise of my creative abilities. The values and needs that I want to bring into more focus in my life include prestige and recognition, intellectual status, job tranquility, knowledge, and leadership.

Functional Skills. My most important functional skills are working with abstract material and concepts, communicating abstract concepts, envisioning the future, writing narratives, and organizing information logically. I am attempting to use these motivated skills in my work by spending as much time as possible writing materials that describe abstract ideas in ways that people can easily grasp them and use them in their own lives. The skills that I need and want to develop to be more successful include acting assertively, managing people, persuading others, allocating resources, and monitoring and regulating workflow.

Adaptive Skills. The personal qualities that work best for me include being ambitious, committed to personal growth, confident, creative, and hardworking. I need to work more on being assertive, demanding of others, methodical, persuasive, and caring.

Internal Barriers. The key barriers that inhibit my success include lack of assertiveness, being reactive instead of proactive, fear of not knowing, impatience, and restlessness. These developmental needs all relate to my need to do a better job building my business and developing and managing the people that work for me.

Mid-Level Corporate Manager

Style. My work type is ESTJ and my style is that of the "fact-minded, practical organizer." I like to organize projects and make sure they are completed. I like being a manager and like to work with people who are focused on getting the job done in a structured environment where there are rewards available for succeeding. I deal with people in a direct way with consistency and fairness. I consider myself to be loyal and dependable.

Career Type. My primary career type is "conventional." I like to be accurate and responsible as well as practical in working and making decisions. I enjoy working on teams and both leading and making a significant contribution. I do not prefer a lot of change in my environment. My secondary career type is "enterprising." I can be aggressive and hard driving when there is a job that needs to get done. I communicate well with my staff. I have always been valued as a key manager in my company where I have worked for over ten years. My tertiary career type is "realistic." I spend my off-work hours in my garden and working around the house, and I take pride in being able to make minor repairs on my own car. At work, I have always been considered to be very practical, "hands-on," and technically capable.

Career Anchor. My primary career anchor is "organizational identity." I have been extremely loyal to my company and consider my career to revolve around being able to do the best job I can do to support my company's success. I have moved four times in ten years in order to do a job that was needed in different divisions in my organization. My secondary career anchor is "functional competence." I tend to be very good at what I do and am interested in excelling and doing the best job I can. I take management training courses whenever possible and have attended major management development programs at universities.

Values and Needs. The most important values and needs currently satisfied in my worklife include affiliation, challenging problems, respect from others, achievement, and security. I would like to see the following values and needs better satisfied in my worklife and need to focus my attention so I can bring these into fruition: prestige/recognition, advancement, challenging problems, independence, and high earnings.

Functional Skills. I consider my top functional skills to be managing people, working effectively on a team, synthesizing facts and ideas, coordinating events and operations, and solving problems. I use these almost every day in my work and have seen significant growth in my mastery of these skills. I need development in acknowledging others, resolving conflict, listening attentively, showing warmth and respect, and operating a computer terminal. I plan to give more attention to these shortcomings through courses and through focusing on developing these skills on the job.

Adaptive Skills. My top adaptive skills include being attentive to details, strong-willed, self-correcting, perceptive, and industrious. These have been extremely useful to me throughout my career not only as a manager, but also when I was working my way up the ladder. I need development in being spontaneous, concerned about people, expressive, dynamic, and open to others. I am uncertain about how to deal with these and will seek professional guidance through coursework or reading.

Internal Barriers. I would like to eliminate or reduce the following internal barriers: lack of diplomacy, stubbornness, impatience, insensitivity to needs and feelings of others, and being confronting to others.

Corporate Administrator

Style. My work type is ISTJ and my style is that of the "analytical manager of facts and details." I am practical, logical, dependable, orderly, matter-of-fact, and well organized. Every job I have has has been one that requires my being well organized and able to work with numbers or other detailed pieces of information that have to be remembered, analyzed, put into the right place, and properly categorized. I get a lot of pleasure from managing in an orderly, well structured, and stable environment without too many surprises.

Career Type. My primary career type is "conventional." I have a small group of long-term close friends with whom I spend time and share common life experiences. I want the people I work with to be orderly and to pay attention to the structure and rules of the organization. I also like my own work to be accurate and practical. I don't like flashy people, ideas, or ways of working. My secondary career type is "investigative." I am analytical in my thinking and enjoy solving problems where I have to use my head to think through the solutions. I have faithful and long-term relationships with a small number of close friends and colleagues. I like to work on teams as long as I am free to make my individual contribution without too much distraction from others. My tertiary career type is "artistic." I read extensively in the arts, attend the theater on a regular basis, and have even acted in community and college theater. When I retire, I would love to be involved in the theater, even as an amateur.

Career Anchor. My primary career anchor is "life-style integration." I am most interested in ensuring that I have a balanced life that includes my interests outside of work, my family, and my friends, and that work doesn't dominate my life. I work hard when I am in the office and do a good job, because I want to be able to feel free and comfortable about pursuing my other interests. My secondary career anchor is "technical/functional competence." I am very interested in being an expert in my field and work and study toward developing a better understanding and more knowledge.

Values and Needs. The most important values and needs currently satisfied in my worklife include order, security, job tranquility, location, and challenging problems. My current job satisfies those needs. They are important enough to me that I would change companies if they could not be satisfied. Those areas that are not yet satisfied include stability, time freedom, working alone, intellectual status, and leisure. I believe that I am working toward the satisfaction of these needs as I grow in my present job and in the company.

Functional Skills. My most important functional skills include administering policy and programs, organizing information logically, negotiating contracts, keeping records, and thinking logically. I use these continuously on my current job and would want to continue using these skills wherever I worked. The functional skills that I consider to be most in need of development include relating to a wide variety of people, communicating effectively, using statistics, delegating responsibility, and resolving conflicts. I also feel that here, as in the values and needs area, that these skills will be developed as I grow in my job and the company.

Adaptive Skills. My most important adaptive skills include being hardworking, organized, self-disciplined, steady, and reliable. I need to work on improving in being more open to others, imaginative, concerned about people, demanding of others, and a better team player.

Internal Barriers. The internal barriers that I feel can hold me back the most and that I need to give attention to overcoming include difficulty with taking criticism, black-or-white thinking, difficulty selling myself, being easily irritated, and inflexibility.

Senior Corporate Manager/ Executive

Style. My work type is ESTJ and my style is that of a "fact-minded, practical organizer." I like to organize people and projects and make sure that they are completed. My prime focus is on getting the job done. I have always been practical, realistic, matter-of-fact, with a natural head for business and leadership. I like projects where the results of my work and my team's efforts are immediate, visible, and tangible. I can be tough when necessary, but I am also objective and logical. I am interested in having people around me who are entirely focused on getting the job done. I believe there should be rewards for meeting goals. I also enjoy community activities when they are meaningful and I have an opportunity to make an important contribution.

Career Type. My primary career type is "enterprising." I have always been drawn to a leadership role in any organization I have been in and consider myself aggressive and self-confident with good social and political skills. I prefer to work in a hard-driving, results-oriented environment with like-minded people. I communicate very effectively and have a wide network of professional colleagues and friends with whom I communicate regularly. My secondary career type is "social." I am active in my community and enjoy working for useful causes. I like to use my leadership abilities to benefit others. I gravitate toward people who match my lifestyle and intellectual interests. My tertiary career type is "conventional." I value economic achievement, material possessions, and status. I like my company to be well organized with structured rules where people are contributing to the overall success of the team.

Career Anchor. My primary career anchor is "managerial competence." My key motivation is to advance up the corporate ladder to higher levels of responsibility, to find opportunities to serve in positions of leadership, to make an increasing contribution to the overall success of the organization, and to have a long-term opportunity for high income and estate-building. I have always worked hard to excel in all three areas of managerial competence and have an MBA as well as a considerable experience with high level management development courses in analytical competence, interpersonal competence, and emotional competence. My secondary career anchor is "pure challenge." I like to win, be successful, overcome obstacles, be the best, be first, beat the competition, and reach for my highest.

Values and Needs. I feel strongly about the following values and diligently maintain them in my worklife: leadership, status, power and authority, profit, gain, and high earnings. The values and needs that I feel are not yet satisfied in my worklife include nurturing and helping others, leisure, prestige and recognition, intellectual status, and adventure/excitement.

Functional Skills. The skills at which I excel and which I feel have allowed me to be successful include acting assertively, influencing others, delegating responsibility, managing people, and making decisions. The functional skills that I am currently working on to improve in my worklife include understanding behavior, listening attentively, reading technical information, showing warmth and support, and writing creatively.

Adaptive Skills. I consider the following adaptive skills as a source of strength: being challenge seeking, imaginative, self-disciplined, resourceful,and a risk-taker. In order to round out my executive abilities, I need to be more encouraging of others, tolerant of others' mistakes, patient, versatile, and expressive.

Internal Barriers. The following barriers have at times kept me from achieving all that I could and will need to be managed more consciously: all-or-nothing behavior, distrust of intuition, inflexible, sense of lack of creativity, and perfectionism.

Secretary

Style. My work type is ISFP and my style is that of an "observant, loyal helper." I am adaptable, caring, cooperative and loyal. I do not like disagreements. I am not interested in dominating or impressing other people. I like to work in a business situation where people are important and where the people I work with go about their business and enjoy it the way I do. I enjoy secretarial work because I can see the results of supporting my boss and working together as team. I work best with a boss who understands me, lets me get my job done and gives me some flexibility in completing my tasks. I also prefer to work in an environment that is reasonably quiet and well-ordered.

Career Type. My primary career type is "social." I am very interested in other people and sensitive to their needs. I like to understand people and help them. I do this both at work and at home with my family. Whenever I have had a choice about where to work I have always chosen a company or a department where people really get along together, are friendly, and help each other. This kind of place is most satisfying for me and working there can be fun. My secondary career type is "conventional." I like the structured, orderly environment of the office of an organized company with clear and well-defined rules and policies. I once worked in an architect's office where everything was very loose. Even though the people were friendly, I couldn't stand the disorganization and had to leave after three months. I am loyal and hard working and can do a great job for a boss who really appreciates me. My tertiary career type is "artistic." I like expressing myself through creative activities including decorating, photography, and sketching with water colors. I like reading about art and architecture, and some of my friends are in the arts.

Career Anchor. My primary career anchor is "sense of service." I enjoy helping and working for others whenever possible. I like to entertain, care for children, and make life easier for a good boss (especially if he or she is important to the company, because I feel like that makes me important to the company). My secondary career anchor is "organizational identity." I like working in a good company that is successful and well thought of by everyone I know. I like the security of belonging to a "family" and have always looked for jobs where the company considered itself to be family. I don't like companies where people are not treated well; I am loyal and want my bosses to recognize that and take care of me. Except for the job in the architect's office that I quit because it was so disorganized, I have worked a long time in one company.

Values and Needs. The things that are most important to me and that I feel really strong about keeping in my work and life are: working with others, helping others, stability, exercising competence, and affiliation. The values and needs that I feel are not yet included enough in my worklife and that I would like to see better developed are achievement, adventure/excitement, helping society, community, and respect from others. I am working to include these things by doing more work as a volunteer and choosing what I think are very good causes to work for in my community.

104

Functional Skills. The things I do best are serving others, showing warmth and support, working effectively on a team, taking quality photographs, and operating a computer terminal. I would like to develop more skill on my job in organizing information logically, evaluating data and ideas, influencing others, interviewing for information, and planning work assignments. I have always tried to develop myself by asking my boss to give me more responsibility and training wherever possible.

Adaptive Skills. The personal qualities that are most important to me and that I think make me a good worker include being able to work well in structured environment, being accurate, having integrity, being friendly, and being hardworking. I need to do better at being assertive, analytical, persistent, risk taking, and tough-minded.

Internal Barriers. My main barriers are difficulty selling myself, feelings of being unsophisticated, lack of assertivenesss, overly trusting, and lack of confidence.

Factory Worker

Style. My work type is ISTP and my style is that of a "practical analyzer." I don't like a line of bull! When people try to convince me of something, it needs to be logical. I like action and I can work hard without getting tired. I am shy except with my family and best friends. I like working in a factory where things get done and everyone is focused on solving problems when they come up. I like to tell the truth about how I see things. I am very loyal to my friends and generous to my family.

Career Type. My primary career type is "realistic." I have good mechanical and athletic ability. I like concrete things like cars and boats and tools and good equipment. I prefer action to words. I like to produce useful things that are well made. I prefer working outdoors when I'm not in the factory. I have had some jobs outdoors and they have been the best ones yet. My secondary career type is "conventional." I like to be precise, well organized, and work in structured situations. I make friends slowly and have a small group of long-term close friends that have the same interests I do. My tertiary career type is "social." I think more people should take responsibility for having their towns work better including the schools and the police and other services. I am active in the local political club and like to have an influence on the way things get done. I also help raise money for the scouts and other groups for kids.

Career Anchor. My primary career anchor is "geographic location." I was born in the town I work in, have all of my friends and family here, and would quit my job before I would leave town. My secondary career anchor is "life-style integration." I am more interested in making sure that I have a balanced life that includes family, friends, hobbies, than have it be just about work. I like to work and think I am good at what I do, but there's more to life than just work.

105

Values and Needs. The most important things to me are location, exercising competence, physical challenge, independence, and job tranquility. What I want more of is play, precision work, making decisions, respect from others, and status. To get these things, I would have to become a supervisor, which I have been avoiding because I am not sure I want too much responsibility at work that might interfere with the rest of my life.

Functional Skills. The skills that I do best are assembling things, diagnosing mechanical problems, using power tools, following instructions, and thinking logically. If I want to be a supervisor I need to be able to lead others, manage people, motivate others, plan work assignments, and maintain schedules. I can take supervisory courses at work if I request them.

Adaptive Skills. I am alert, conscientious, self-starting, physically strong, and industrious. I need to be more motivated, open to ideas, ambitious, encouraging of others, and people-oriented.

Internal Barriers. I feel blocked by my fear of taking responsibility, being naive politically, having poor listening skills, being confronting to others, and having a low frustration tolerance.

Independent Corporate Contributor

Style. My work type is INTP and my style is that of an "inquisitive analyzer." I am intensely analytical and objectively critical. I am mainly interested in ideas, very curious, and can't stand small talk. I learn very quickly, am insightful, intellectually curious, persevering, thorough, and have sharply defined interests. I like an unstructured environment and like to work independently in solving thorny technical problems. I love logic and enjoy long, detailed arguments.

Career Type. My primary career type is "investigative." I am analytical, comfortable with abstractions and prefer to cope with life and its problems by analytical thinking. I am scholarly, self-confident, and have scientific and mathematical ability. I like to work in a quiet and scholarly environment where I can pursue my work without interference and where there are plenty of intellectual resources like computers, laboratories and libraries that I can use whenever I feel like – night or day. My friends are mostly people I work with. My secondary career type is "artistic." I play the piano and am a fairly competent amateur potter. I love music and feel a tremendous sense of self-expression when I am playing the piano or working with clay on my wheel. If I didn't have to make a living working in a company, I would stay at home and read, play music, and make pottery. That would make me very happy. None of the other career types seem to apply to me.

Career Anchor. My primary career anchor is "technical/functional competence." I am very dedicated to being an outstanding contributor in my field and being recognized as such. I wouldn't mind getting a Nobel prize if they gave one in my specialty. The only thing I am interested in at work is getting as good as I can at what I do and being the company's leading expert in it. I would like to produce a body of work that is useful and outstanding. My secondary career anchor is "pure challenge." I love to solve the toughest problems, be the first to invent or discover something, and really test my wits and skills against other people or just against my own abilities. I'm a very good chess and I-go player.

Values and Needs. The values and needs that are most important in my life, that are currently at a level that I find acceptable, and without which I would not be willing to work are creative expression, achievement, challenging problems, independence, and intellectual status. I definitely want more fame, prestige/recognition, variety, time freedom, and work on the frontiers of knowledge.

Functional Skills. The areas where I really excel at work are analyzing facts and ideas, conceiving, creating, and developing ideas, gathering information and data, perceiving and defining cause and effect relationships, and synthesizing facts and ideas. The skills that I need to develop more are tuning in to needs and feelings of others, working effectively on a team, working within a structure, maintaining schedules, and following through. I think I need these because my growth as a contributor will require that I work more with others to develop and implement major projects.

Adaptive Skills. The adaptive skills that work best for me are concentration, being demanding of self, being intelligent, being methodical, and being a quick learner. In order to become more successful at creating and developing more important contributions, I will need to develop myself to be more supportive of others, resilient, diplomatic, able to use time effectively, and empathetic.

Internal Barriers. I need to handle the following barriers: difficulty managing time, becoming easily bored, impatience, being insensitive to the needs and feelings of others, and being stubborn.

***Graduate
Student***

Style. My work type is ENTJ and my style is that of the "intuitive innovative organizer." I have always enjoyed being a leader, taking charge, being assertive, and taking command of any situation I am in. I am well-informed, read a lot, and like to learn new things. I like to work around people who want to get things done, and I have little patience with inefficiency.

Career Type. My primary career type is "enterprising." I place a high value on political and economic matters and am drawn to power and leadership roles. I am assertive and self-confident. I like working with hard-driving people who are dedicated to achieving bottom-line results. I worked all through college in a student business and excelled at sales and marketing. I rose to the head of the business in my senior year and realized that I could have a good career in business, as a leader or executive. My secondary career type is "investigative." I am analytical and comfortable with abstractions. I consider myself original in my thinking. I prefer strong intellectual discussions about things that interest me and avoid small talk unless it is politically useful. I gravitate toward people who match my lifestyle and interests. My tertiary career type is artistic. I like the theater, the opera, and the ballet. I spend time at museums and have taken several art history courses.

Career Anchor. My primary career anchor is "managerial competence." My prime motivation is to advance up a corporate ladder to higher levels of responsibility. When I finish my MBA, I intend to get into a dynamic organization that is growing into a big future and needs people who are ambitious and energetic and want to be leaders. I know that I will need to develop myself in all three areas of managerial competence – analytical, interpersonal, and emotional. I think I have a good start on the first. My secondary career anchor is "autonomy/independence." I think this will point me toward working in a smaller company where I will have a chance to express myself fully earlier in my career. I will probably also want to consider an entrepreneurial opportunity at some point in my career.

Values and Needs. The values and needs that are most important to me and that I will be looking for on my first job are challenging problems, adventure/excitement, fast pace, making decisions, and respect from others. The values and needs that I will be seeking as I get more experience in the business world include profit, gain, power and authority, status, independence, and creative expression.

Functional Skills. My most important functional skills are acting assertively, leading others, analyzing facts and ideas, presenting information logically, and understanding complex materials. The functional skills I think I need to work on to be successful in business are influencing others, relating to a wide variety of people, designing and developing systems, acknowledging, and managing budgets.

Adaptive Skills. My key personal qualities which I think will be valuable in my career include intelligence, being industrious, being aggressive, being goal-oriented, and having a strong-will. I will need to improve myself in the areas of flexibility, being open to others, being considerate, being empathetic, and being able to admit mistakes.

Internal Barriers. I want to eliminate these barriers that I think could inhibit my success in business: arrogance, being easily irritated, being slow to see humor, impatience, inflexibility.

University Professor

Style. My work type is ENFJ and my style is that of an "imaginative harmonizer and worker with people." I am concerned with what others think or want and try to handle things with regard for other people's feelings. I am loyal to my institution and to people that I respect. I am a good teacher because I am at my best when speaking in front of groups. I put a lot of time into my work and am caring, tolerant, trustworthy, concerned and nurturing.

Career Type. My primary career type is "investigative." I am analytical, comfortable with abstractions and prefer to handle problems through the use of analytical thinking. I consider myself to be highly original, and have excellent verbal and mathematical skills. My secondary career type is "social." I am a good teacher because I have a high interest in other people and am sensitive to their needs. I value interpersonal relations and use my social skills and verbal abilities to influence my students. My tertiary career type is "artistic." I play the violin, spend time listening to music at home and going to concerts. I consider myself to be creative, expressive, and imaginative. I can express my ideas with emotion and strength and am a good writer.

Career Anchor. My primary career anchor is "technical/functional competence." I am strongly motivated toward expertise in my professional field and strive to produce high quality work. My self concept has a lot to do with my reputation as an expert in my field. My secondary career type is "autonomy/independence." I like to do things in my own way and in my own time. One of the reasons I chose to teach in a university is that I can work quite independently of others, at my own pace, and on problems that I consider to be important.

Values and Needs. The most important values and needs that are currently satisfied in my role as a faculty member at a prestigious university are achievement, creative expression, intellectual status, working on frontiers of knowledge, and independence. Those values and needs that I would most like to expand in my worklife include high earnings, help society, artistic creativity, change and variety, and prestige and recognition. I am getting more of these values and needs into my life by writing a book and by attempting to expand the amount of consulting and lecturing that I do around the country.

Functional Skills. My outstanding functional skills are teaching, communicating effectively, analyzing facts and ideas, presenting information logically, researching subjects, and playing a musical instrument. The functional skills that I would most like to improve for both work and pleasure include planning projects, managing budgets, criticizing constructively, operating a computer terminal, and maintaining physical stamina.

Adaptive Skills. The adaptive skills that I think are most important to me and that are currently at an acceptable level are clear thinking, being independent, being intelligent, being tenacious, and being inventive. The most important adaptive skills that I think are currently in need of development include being able to deliver on time, diplomatic, politically aware, organized, demanding of others, and having high energy.

Internal Barriers. The following internal barriers should be reduced or eliminated: fear of financial insecurity, difficulty managing stress and pressure, being cynical and skeptical, impatience, lack of diplomacy, and restlessness.

Human Resource Professional

Style. My work type is ENFP and my style is that of a "warmly enthusiastic planner of change." I am high-spirited, imaginative and able to do almost anything that interests me. I like to solve the problems that people have and am innovative and can see new ways of doing things. I have a lot of energy and initiative and use my feeling judgment to add depth to my insights. I like to work in an organization where there are not too many constraints and where my colleagues are imaginative and the work is concentrated on expanding human potential. I am a good networker and work hard to keep up with both friends and colleagues. I am sympathetic to others and have good insights into other people's personal problems.

Career Type. My primary career type is "social." I have a high interest in people and have based my career on working with people to help them improve their potential. My secondary career type is "investigative." I am interested in analyzing things although I would not want my whole job to be about facts and figures. I do have an analytical mind and like to use it in solving problems. I love a good intellectual discussion about things that interest me, especially when they concern how people behave at work and how that behavior can be modified or improved. My tertiary career type is "enterprising." I am adventurous and persuasive. I am popular, assertive, and self-confident and enjoy leadership roles. I have lots of professional and personal relationships.

Career Anchor. My primary career anchor is "sense of service." My work has to do with serving people so that they can become better at what they do and be more satisfied in their work and their lives. I chose the field of human resources because I wanted to be involved in working with people and wanted to be able to express myself in a wide variety of ways. My secondary career anchor is "functional competence." I want to be as good as possible at what I do and be considered an expert in my field. I study a lot, go to conferences and seminars, and try to spend time with other experts. I would rather leave my organization than be promoted into a position that did not let me exercise my professional skills and continue to work at my career.

Values and Needs. The most important values and needs that are currently satisfied in my worklife include knowledge, helping others, working with others, exercising competence, and independence. The values and needs that are currently not fully satisfied and that I would like to include in my life are challenging problems, advancement, prestige and recognition, helping society, and high earnings.

Functional Skills. The functional skills that I use the most on my job and that I enjoy using are motivating others, tuning in to the needs and feelings of others, training people, coordinating events and operations, and presenting information logically. The functional skills that I would most like to improve are promoting ideas, managing conflict, maintaining schedules, understanding complex materials, and writing creatively. Improving these skills would allow me to be a more independent producer of results.

Adaptive Skills. My most important adaptive skills currently at an acceptable level are being purposeful, dedicated to personal goals, dependable, spontaneous, and people-oriented. I need development in self-discipline, being firm, being a risk-taker, being challenge-seeking, and being systematic.

Internal Barriers. The internal barriers that most inhibit my success include having conflicting values, fear of looking foolish, low stress tolerance, being overly trusting, and being restless.

110

[√] *Writing a Detailed Personal Career Profile*

Inconsistencies and Uncertainty

*I*f you read the first example (page 99) carefully, it will strike you that there are some inconsistencies between various sections. For example, in the section on career types, the writer (a male) says that he considers himself aggressive and self-confident. Yet, in the section on internal barriers, he says that lack of assertiveness is a key barrier that he needs to work on for more satisfaction and success. These seemingly contradictory statements point out an important function of the *Personal Career Profile*. Human beings are not perfectly definable and consistent in their behavior, in their understanding of themselves (and each other), and in the predictability of their future thoughts, actions, and feelings – regardless of how sophisticated or comprehensive an assessment is made. Where inconsistencies arise, they signal areas in which the uncertainty of accurately and comprehensively predicting the whole truth about who we "really" are becomes evident.

These areas of uncertainty are worth further exploration and thought, and where they occur, you are encouraged to delve deeper. You can explore further by reading some of the materials suggested in previous chapters, by spending more time thinking about the issues involved, by revisiting some of the assessments you did in this book, by discussing your profile with friends, family, peers, subordinates, your boss, or others who know you well, or through counseling or therapy.

Giving the Profile Reality and Integrity

*I*t is suggested that you write your drafts on a word processor if you have access to one. You will want to be able to revise your drafts as easily as possible. When you finish a draft, read it over more than once. Make it work for you. Make it real for you. Revise it until it tells the truth about you in a way that you recognize yourself and can say…"That is definitely me!" When you can do that, your level of certainty and satisfaction will be high, and you will be better able to know yourself and work toward being able to…

"…be who you are."

Instructions for Completing Your Detailed Personal Career Profile

*R*efer to the examples for clarification of any of these instructions. Use your *Concise Personal Profile* for quick retrieval of information. Write as much as you feel necessary to describe yourself fully and with satisfaction.

1. Style. Use your own words to paraphrase the material that describes your psychological type and style in the chapter on Style. Write only those portions of the description that you feel apply to you. Add any additional ideas, thoughts, or feelings that you have about your type.

2. Career Types. Use your own words to paraphrase the material that describes your primary, secondary, and tertiary Career Types in the chapter on Career Types. Write only those portions of the description that you feel apply to you. Add any additional ideas, thoughts, or feelings that you have about your types.

3. Career Anchor. Use your own words to paraphrase the material that describes your primary and secondary Career Anchor in the chapter on Motivation. Write only those portions of the description that you feel apply to you. Add any additional ideas, thoughts, or feelings that you have about your anchor.

4. Values and Needs. Write a sentence that states your five most important values and needs. Add a statement about what you are doing to include those values in your worklife. Then, write a sentence that states your five most important values and needs not yet satisfied. You may also want to add a statement about your level of satisfaction or dissatisfaction about how well you feel these values are reflected in your worklife. Add any additional ideas, thoughts, or feelings that you have about your values and needs.

5. Functional Skills. Write a sentence that states your five most important people, data, and thing skills that you currently consider to be at an acceptable level of development. Then write a sentence that states the five most important people, data, and thing skills that you feel are currently in need of development. Add any additional thoughts, ideas, or feelings that you may have about your functional skills.

6. Adaptive Skills. Write a sentence that states your five most important adaptive skills/personal qualities that you currently consider to be at an acceptable level of development. Then write a sentence that states the five most important adaptive skills that you feel are currently in need of development. Add any additional thoughts, ideas, or feelings that you may have about your adaptive skills.

7. Internal Barriers. Write a sentence that states the five most important internal barriers that you feel are currently in need of reduction or elimination for more success and satisfaction in your worklife.

[√] *Applications*   *8*

*I*f you have completed all of the exercises in this book, you have probably already discovered the satisfaction in knowing more about yourself. In addition to this subjective benefit, there are practical applications in which the information can be used.

<table>
<tr>
<td>

Career Development Planning

</td>
<td>

*E*very good career development process begins with a foundation of clear self-knowledge. All of the information developed in these exercises will be useful in selecting a career, planning a career path, advancing a career, determining the development you need to follow a specific career, moving into a new job that fits you well, or improving your performance on the job you are in. The remaining steps in these processes include:

1. Investigating the opportunities available for expanding the application of your skills and interests on your current job, in a new position in your organization, or in a new career or organization.

2. Targeting a specific opportunity that you think would be satisfying and practical, and would represent a good fit for you.

3. Developing a complete plan for taking advantage of that new opportunity. Remember, the new opportunity may be expanding your contribution on the job you are in now, on a new job in your organization, or in a different organization or career.

4. Implementing your plan and managing your ongoing career.

Any of the books referenced in the General Career Planning section of Chapter 9 will give you a more detailed description of this process.

</td>
</tr>
<tr>
<td>

Preparing Resumes and Interviews

</td>
<td>

*T*he information and understanding you have developed here will also be useful to you in writing resumes and preparing for various kinds of interviews. In particular, it is valuable to be very clear about your style, skills, and developmental needs when holding either a career discussion or performance appraisal meeting with your manager. If you are interviewing for a new position in your present organization, or for a new job in a new company, it will also be very useful to reread your *Personal Career Profile* and become familiar with your skills, style, and other attributes. This information will allow you to give more accurate, complete, and self-assured answers to questions that may be asked by an interviewer.

</td>
</tr>
</table>

Personal Growth and Development

*M*any people are interested and active in their own personal development whether it is job and career related or simply to improve the quality of their lives. Much of what you have learned about yourself in doing these exercises will apply in many areas of your life. In general, greater appreciation of self and the building of your self-esteem are available. In particular, the psychological type and style assessed in Chapter 2, the adaptive skills (personal qualities) from Chapter 5, and the internal barriers from Chapter 6 apply across your life and will give you considerable insight into lifestyle issues and problems with which you may be wrestling. While this work is not intended to be a substitute for professional support, it will be useful in illuminating issues to which you might wish to give your attention with or without a professional.

Interpersonal Communication and Relationships

*O*ut of your own self-exploration, you should have become aware of the differences among people and the value of the many behavioral preferences and styles, skills, career types, career anchors, and other charatceristics. This insight leads to better understanding and should improve your ability to accept individual differences and work with others, not only your boss, colleagues, and subordinates, but also in the other relationships in your life including family and friends.

Some of the references in Chapter 9 will provide important information about using the insight you have gained here in expanding, improving, and mastering your communications and relationships.

Counseling and Therapy

*T*he information developed here may also be useful to a professional counselor or therapist with whom you may be working. The greater depth of insight into your self-concept, sense of identity, style, motivations, strengths and weaknesses, internal barriers, and development needs can provide opportunity for fruitful discussions with your counselor or therapist. The material is useful to enlarge and reinforce your own sense of identity and self acceptance. Some counselors or therapists may welcome this additional data. The use of such materials is a highly individual preference, and the best advice is to follow the lead of your counselor or therapist.

Finding a Career Counselor

*S*everal organizations can be helpful to you in locating a professional and accredited career counselor or counseling agency close to where you live or work.

International Association of Counseling Services, Inc. (IACS), 5999 Stevenson Avenue, Suite 307, Alexandria, VA 22304, (703) 823-9800. The IACS accredits career counseling agencies throughout the United States and Canada. The organization sets high professional standards and helps publicize agencies that are competent and reliable. For a list of accredited agencies in your area, send a stamped, self-addressed envelope to IACS.

National Board for Certified Counselors (NBCC), 5999 Stevenson Avenue, Suite 307, Alexandria, VA 22304, (703) 461-6222. The NBCC is a not-for-profit organization that certifies individual career counselors regardless of organizational affiliation. For a list of certified career counselors in your area and a copy of NBCC's consumer guidelines for selecting a career counselor, send a double-stamped, self-addressed envelope to NBCC.

A Final Word

*I*t is important to recognize that the process of self development and growth is highly complex. Changing behavior is never an easy process. It requires that you first become aware of those aspects of your behavior that you wish to change before appropriate steps can be taken.

This book will help you to get more in touch with both your strengths and your developmental needs. As a result of your efforts in completing the exercises in the book you will achieve the following:

1. *A clearer and more expanded definition of yourself in terms of both your strengths and developmental needs which will help build your self-esteem and enhance your self-acceptance.*

2. *A greater ability to make more effective job and career decisions.*

3. *An enhanced ability to improve personal and professional effectiveness.*

Accept and nourish your true self.

[√]*Suggestions for Further Reading*

*T*he field of careers, jobs, worklife, and the assessment of people's style and skills, types, motivation, and values, and all of the other factors related to people at work has received significant attention from hundreds of authors.

General Comments About the Literature

*C*onsidering the importance of these issues to each of us, surprisingly few books have made it to any kind of best-seller list. The books described below are a small sample of what is available, but enough to give you a deeper appreciation and insight into the purposes of the assessments through which you have gone in this book.

Style

*A*n enormous amount of material, has been written about psychological type and style particularly in connection with the Myers-Briggs Type Indicator, including books, pamphlets, Ph.D. theses, technical papers and journal articles, and proprietary consulting documents. A few of the available and more readable and useful books and materials are described here. Each of these in turn can lead you to additional materials if you wish to develop a deeper interest in the subject.

1. ***Introduction to Type, A description of the theory and applications of the Myers-Briggs Type Indicator,*** by Isabel Briggs Myers, Consulting Psychologists Press, 577 College Avenue, Palo Alto, CA 94306, Fourth Edition, 1987.

   This 32-page booklet contains an excellent and readable introduction to the theory of types and a detailed description of each of the types and styles. A short section is included on applications of type and style in relationships, career choices, the effects of each preference in work situations and the use of type to improve problem solving.

2. ***Introduction to Type in Organizational Settings***, by Sandra Krebs Hirsh and Jean M. Kummerow, Consulting Psychologists Press, 577 College Avenue, Palo Alto, CA 94306, 1987.

   Also a 32-page booklet, this document contains brief descriptions of the 16 types with material on the effects of preferences in work situations, preferred methods of communication for each of the preferences, and, for each four-letter type, points on their contributions to organizations, leadership style, preferred work environment, potential pitfalls, and suggestions for development.

3. ***Please Understand Me, Character & Temperament Types***, by David Keirsey and Marilyn Bates, distributed by Prometheus Nemesis Book Company, PO Box 2748, Del Mar, CA 92014, Fourth Edition ©1984 Gnosology Books Ltd.

A readable, interesting, and informative paperback dealing with a variety of issues concerning psychological type and style. The book includes The Keirsey Temperament Sorter, another assessment tool that also leads to a determination of the 16 psychological types using the Myers-Briggs extension of Jungian typology. Long and detailed descriptions of each of the types are given, and information on style is included with regard to life-mates, temperament in children, temperament in leading, and some statements about career and job preferences, and work style.

4. ***Gifts Differing***, by Isabel Briggs Myers with Peter B. Myers, Consulting Psychologists Press, 577 College Avenue, Palo Alto, CA 94306, © 1980.

In paperback format, this warm and moving book describes the history of the work of Katherine Briggs and her daughter Isabel Briggs Myers in the extension of Jungian typology and the development of the MBTI. The 16 types are described in considerable detail, and the complementary nature of preferences and types is extremely well developed. Some discussion is given to the relationship of each type to worklife, including a chapter on Type and Occupation. Chapters on applications also include Use of the Opposites, Type and Marriage, Type and Early Learning, and Learning Styles.

5. ***People Types & Tiger Stripes, A Practical Guide to Learning Styles***, by Gordon Lawrence, Center for Applications of Psychological Type, Inc., Gainesville, FL, Second Edition, ©1982.

A 100-page paperback which includes Introduction to Type (see reference 1 above), this book probes the relationship between type and learning styles. Materials are included on using types in planning instruction, developmental needs and type concepts, type and teaching styles, and type and learning styles.

6. ***Type Talk***, by Otto Kroeger and Janet Thuesen, Delacorte Press, New York, NY, 1988.

The authors have developed a popular guide on how to understand your personality type with applications to your work life and your personal and parent/child relationships. This book will help you to better understand who you are, why you do the things you do, and how to better understand and relate to those around you by appreciating individual differences in style.

118

Career Type (Holland Typology)

*T*he Holland typology (R-I-A-S-E-C) has also received tremendous attention since its introduction, and there is hardly a publication on jobs or careers that does not at least mention the typology, if not use it extensively. Again, only a few books are mentioned here that deal with Career Types. They in turn will lead you to more if you care to dig deeper.

1. ***Making Vocational Choices: A Theory of Careers***, by John L. Holland, Prentice-Hall, Englewood Cliffs, NJ, 1985.

   An expanded revision of Holland's original 1966 *The Psychology of Vocational Choice*, this book provides a detailed background for the Holland typology including both theoretical and practical considerations.

2. ***Coming Alive From Nine To Five, The Career Search Handbook***, by Betty Neville Michelozzi, Mayfield Publishing Company, 1240 Villa Street, Mountain View, CA 94041, Third Edition, 1988.

   An extremely thorough, 300-page large-format paperback that deals in depth with the subject of job motivation. Including dozens of inventories, exercises, and other materials that help the reader to discover their "job satisfiers," the discussion of the Holland types is outstanding. The book also includes excellent chapters on job-finding and the job market for the late '80s and the '90s.

3. ***Taking Charge of Your Career Direction***, by Robert D. Lock, Brooks/Cole Publishing Company, Pacific Grove, CA, ©1988 Wadsworth, Inc.

   This 375 page large-format paperback has the depth and detail of a textbook and is useful for the extent of its various assessments and exercises. The book includes tables of educational majors classified by Holland types, as well as other information about jobs, careers, and the Holland types. The author does a particularly excellent job in dealing with work values, including assessment and inventory exercises.

4. ***If you don't know where you're going, you'll probably end up somewhere else***, by David Campbell, Ph.D., Argus Communications, One DLM Park, Allen, TX 75002, 1974.

   This 144 page, pocket-sized paperback is written to be read in one easy sitting and is filled with amusing drawings, sayings, and an effective message about lifework planning. The section on the Holland types is succinct and informative.

5. ***Dictionary of Holland Occupational Codes***, compiled by Gary D. Gottfredson, John L. Holland, and Deborah Kimiko Ogawa, Consulting Psychologists Press, Inc., 577 College Avenue, Palo Alto, CA 94306, 1982.

Almost 500 pages in a paperback format, this massive volume contains a comprehensive cross-index of Holland's RIASEC codes with 12,000 occupations from the *Dictionary of Occupational Titles.* The book also contains a 23-page description of the theoretical and technical origins of the work as well as a detailed bibliography of materials on occupational research and applications. A new edition will be published in 1989.

Career Anchors

1. ***Career Anchors: Discovering Your Real Values***, by Edgar H. Schein, University Associates, Inc., 8517 Production Avenue, San Diego, CA 92121, 1985.

A 50-page large format paperback, this work contains a Career Anchor assessment and detailed descriptions of each of the eight anchors. Written by the originator of the Career Anchor concept, the book is readable and useful for gaining a deeper insight into the meaning of a specific anchor.

2. ***Career Dynamics: Matching Individual and Organizational Needs***, by Edgar H. Schein, Addison-Wesley Publishing Company, Inc., Reading, MA, 1978.

A comprehensive presentation of Schein's work in career development, this book includes material on Career Anchors, individual development, the individual-organization interaction, and managing human resource planning and development.

3. ***Managing the New Careerists***, by C. Brooklyn Derr, Jossey-Bass Publishers, 350 Sansome Street, San Francisco, CA 94104, 1986.

Influenced by Schein's work, the author shows managers and others how to use information about employees' career orientation to improve job-person fit, increase productivity, and reduce turnover. He presents the five distinct orientations among today's employees - getting secure, getting ahead, getting free, getting high, and getting balanced - and describes the needs, talents, and values of employees with each orientation.

Skills Identification

1. ***The Three Boxes of Life, And How To Get Out of Them***, by Richard N. Bolles, Ten Speed Press, Box 7123, Berkeley, CA 94707, 1981.

Written by America's best know author on careers and jobs, this book provides a stimulating exploration of the art and technology of creating a balanced life. This paperback volume of almost 500 pages provides good job-search material as well as an excellent and detailed section on the Holland types and their relationship to work and specific occupations.

Other books by the same author and publisher include *What Color Is Your Parachute* and *Where Do I Go From Here With My Life.*

2. ***The New Quick Job-Hunting Map,*** by Richard N. Bolles, Ten Speed Press, Box 7123, Berkeley, CA 94707, 1989.

   This highly readable and useable pamphlet provides an excellent group of skill identification exercises including functional, specific content, and adaptive skills.

3. ***Your Hidden Skills,*** by Henry C. Pearson, Moury Press, Wayland, MA, 1981.

   The author describes a method for identifying the skills you already possess but are not fully aware of. Twelve clearly defined steps (with forms) help you develop a pattern of your key talents plus solid proof that you already use them effectively. The book is based on a process initiated at Polaroid Corporation and developed by the author over a seven year period in both corporate and non-corporate settings.

4. ***The Complete Job-Search Handbook,*** by Howard Figler, Ph.D., Henry Holt and Company, Inc., 115 West 18th Street, New York, NY 10011, 1988.

   Figler is one of the most articulate writers in the career field and has done an excellent job in providing a series of discussions and exercises on motivation, values, and skills in this paper-back of almost 400 pages. His work on values is particularly good, and the discussion of skills is outstanding.

General Career Planning

1. ***The Salaried Professional, How to Make the Most of Your Career***, Joseph A. Raelin, Praeger Publishers, 521 Fifth Avenue, New York, NY 10175, 1948.

   A detail-packed paper-back of almost 300 pages, this volume provides one of the few discussions of the relationship among psychological type, Career Anchors, Career Types, values, skills, and the other indicators of people's relationship to their worklives. Fully referenced, this book also includes inventories and exercises useful to career exploration and to understanding ways of excelling in a job and effectively managing and developing a career.

2. ***Taking Charge of Your Career Direction***, by Robert D. Lock, Brooks/Cole Publishing Company, Pacific Grove, CA, 1988.

   Highly readable and thorough, this book contains an excellent set of inventories and exercises on interests, skills, motivations, and work values. The final chapters provide materials on narrowing your occupational prospects, making career decisions, and reality testing your career choice.

3. ***The Inventurers, Excursions in Life and Career Renewal***, by Janet Hagber and Richard Leider, Addison-Wesley Publishing Company, Reading, MA, 1982.

The authors define an "inventurer" as "…someone who is willing to take a long look at yourself and consider new options, venture inward, and explore." An unusual book, this work takes a holistic approach to career planning including mind, body, and spirit. The volume contains material on life stages and styles, work styles, and a formatted process for making choices about these critical issues, including exercises and inventories.

4. ***Your Career: Choices, Chances, Changes***, by David C. Borchard, John J. Kelly, and Nancy Pat K. Weaver, Kendall Hunt Publishing Company, Dubuque, IA, 1984.

A 300-page large format paperback, this comprehensive workbook contains a full career planning process including inventories, assessments, and exercises. Information is also included on organizing small discussion groups, conducting career information interviews, and other materials useful to both the career planner and the career facilitator, instructor, or counselor.

Management Development

1. ***Successful Manager's Handbook, Development Suggestions for Today's Manager***, edited by Brian L. Davis, Ph.D., Lowell W. Hellervik, Ph.D., and James L. Sheard, Ph.D., Personnel Decisions, Inc., 2000 Plaza VII Tower, 45 South Seventh Street, Minneapolis, MN 55402-1606, Third Edition, 1989.

This may be the outstanding management development material publicly available. A large format paperback of over 450 pages, this volume contains extremely detailed developmental exercises, tips, advice, and other useful information for the personal development of anyone interested in becoming an excellent manager. Administrative, leadership, interpersonal, communication, and cognitive skills are all covered in detail, along with personal adaptability, personal motivation, and occupational/technical knowledge.

2. ***Social Skills***, by Robert Bolton, Touchstone Books, New York, NY, 1986.

This communication handbook deals with roadblocks to communication, the ability to listen, asserting yourself, resolving conflicts, and working out problems with others. Both thought provoking and practical, it is filled with workable ideas that can be used to improve your communication in meaningful ways.

3. ***High Performance Leadership – Strategies for Maximum Productivity***, by Philip Harris, Scott Foresman & Company, Glenview, IL, 1989.

The author is a behavioral psychologist and top management consultant. In this book, he provides an in-depth exploration of the skills that managers must have in order to create a maximum performance environment. The book includes a wealth of ideas and resources for managers to use in developing skills for coping with changing organizations. An excellent appendix of resources is provided.

4. ***Social Style/Management Style: Developing Productive Working Relationships***, by Robert Bolton and Dorothy Grover Bolton, Amacon Books, American Management Association, Washington, D.C., 1984.

Are you an Amiable, an Analytical, an Expressive, or a Driver? This book shows you how to recognize your particular style and use that knowledge to manage others more effectively, increase creativity and set appropriate life goals.

Internal Barriers - Personal Growth and Development

Although books like those discussed below are not a substitute for working with a professional counselor or therapist on internal barriers, they can be useful in raising the level of your awareness and expanding your perspective, as well as providing useful strategies and techniques for coping more effectively with barriers. Many people in the course of engageing in this self exploratory process become aware of issues and feelings that are best handled with a professional therapist. For those who would like further guidance in selecting a therapist please see reference #10.

1. ***Your Perfect Right***, by Robert E. Alberti and Michael Emmons, Impact Publishers, 1988.

This book is a classic in the assertiveness training field. This newest edition is totally revised and expanded and includes excellent new chapters on goal-setting and on-the-job assertiveness. This book can help you to express yourself positively and respect others at the same time.

2. ***The Plateauing Trap***, by Judith Bardwick, Bantam Books, New York, NY, 1986.

Do you ever feel as if your career is at a stand-still - that your work has lost its challenge and your life has become a tedious routine? If so, you may have fallen into the plateauing trap. The author, a psychologist and leading management consultant discusses how to escape the pitfalls of the trap and revitalize your career. Practical strategies are discussed to enable you to create a fresh opportunity for personal growth and positive change. The book includes an excellent discussion on how to create a balance between your personal and professional life.

3. *Feeling Good – The New Mood Therapy*, by David D. Burns, Wukkuan Morris & Co., New York, NY, 1980.

This is the first major book written for the general public to introduce the principles of cognitive therapy. The book teaches us that by changing the way we think about things, we can alter our moods, deal with emotionally upsetting problems, and reduce depression and anxiety. In clear, simple language, the author outlines a systematic program for controlling thought distortions that lead to pessimism, low self-esteem, anger, guilt, and other common difficulties of daily living. The book includes an excellent discussion of ways to overcome perfectionism.

4. *Overcoming Procrastination*, by Albert Ellis and William Knaus, NAL Penguin Co., New York, NY 1977.

One of the first and certainly one of the best books to focus specifically on helping people gain insight into the reasons why they procrastinate and to develop strategies and tactics for dealing with the problem. The book uses the techniques of rational emotive therapy and combines cognitive, behavioral, and emotive methods for overcoming procrastination.

5. *When Smart People Fail*, by Carol Hyatt and Linda Gottlieb, Penguin Group, New York, NY, 1980.

This book is filled with positive, reassuring advice regarding how defeats are not only survivable but how they can be stepping stones for renewed success. The authors focus solely on career failure. They investigate the process of coping with setbacks and taking advantage of options. The book outlines the phases of career failure and discusses the nine most common reasons for failure – poor interpersonal skills, mismatch of abilities, mismatch of personalities, mismatch of styles, mismatch of values, lack of commitment, sex discrimination, race discrimination, and age discrimination.

6. *Self-Esteem*, by Matt McKay and Pat Fanning, St. Martins Press, New York, NY 1987.

This book provides a valuable discussion of tactics and strategies for constructing or renovating the foundation of your self-esteem. It includes material to help you discover which of your "personal rules" and "shoulds" are healthy and which cause conflict, guilt, and negative reactions.

124

7. ***Overcoming Indecisiveness***, by Theodore Rubin, Harper & Row, New York, NY, 1985.

   Rubin reveals a step-by-step attack on indecisiveness that can also result in strengthening your sense of self. This book provides useful ideas and strategies for anyone having trouble making up their minds.

8. ***Taking Care of Business — A Psychiatrist's Guide for True Career Success***, by David Viscott, Pocket Books, Inc., New York, NY, 1985.

   The better you manage people and yourself, the more, the author believes, you will succeed in a career. In this humane and down-to-earth guide, Dr. Viscott shows you how to develop the personal insights and the communication skills vital to achieving your professional goals. Powerful techniques are provided to help you read people clearly, recognize your own talents, and negotiate successfully. A particularly useful section is the discussion on how to recognize three main personality types – dependent, controlling, and competitive - and how to respond to each constructively.

9. ***How To Be Organized In Spite Of Yourself***, by S. Schlesenger and R. Roesch, NAL Books, New York, 1989.

   This is an excellent book dealing with issues of time management, space management, improving organization and reducing clutter. The authors have devised personalized solutions that provide ten different systems to match ten different personality types.

10. ***Making Therapy Work: Your Guide to Choosing, Using, and Ending Therapy***, by F. Gordon, B. Gangi, and G. Wallman, Harper and Row Publishers, New York, 1988.

    For all those considering working with a professional therapist, this is a hands-on guide to getting the most out of individual, group, or family counseling. The authors cover basic consumer advice in finding the right kind of psychotherapy for you including how to choose among different schools of therapy. The book also discusses such topics as taking stock of your life, building a good working relationship with your therapist that meets your needs, overcoming obstacles to change, and knowing what to do when someone you care about needs help. A rich resource section is included with recommended readings, referral organizations, and hot lines.

About the Author

*G*erald M. Sturman, Ph.D. is Chairman & CEO of The Career Development Team, a national corporate training firm. CDT designs, develops, and delivers a wide variety of programs and products in the career management field used extensively by major corporations across the United States.

A successful career-changer, Dr. Sturman taught engineering at M.I.T. and Columbia, was a partner in a major international engineering firm, and now heads his own organization in the area of human resources.

Dr. Sturman is the author of *Managing Your Career With "POWER,"* also published by Bierman House.